COMMONWEALTH OF PENNSYLVANIA

Health Care Fraud: A Rising Threat

Pennsylvania Crime Commission

ISBN 0-937972-02-9

Printed in the Commonwealth of Pennsylvania

523 E. Lancaster Ave.
Post Office Box 45
St. Davids, PA 19087
(215) 687-6500

Pennsylvania Crime Commission

Alvin B. Lewis, Jr., Esq., Chairman

Clifford C. Cooper, Esq.
Thomas F. Lamb, Esq.
Malcolm L. Lazin, Esq.
Dean Roach

Wallace P. Hay, Executive Director

Donald Johnson, Esq., Deputy Executive Director/Chief Counsel

Staff
Sharon Beerman
Frank Booth
Carl Brown
Deborah Brown
Nancy Checket
Vincent Clemente
Eileen Commons
Tom Connor
John Contino, Esq.
Willie C. Byrd
Wendy D'Agostino
Michael D'Aniello
Christopher DeCree
Victor DiCicco
John Ditmore
Daniel Fedeanis
William Foran
William J. Fry, III
Donna Groom
Michael Hoey
Oliver Hunter
James Kanavy
Lee Kautzman
Steven Keller
Gregory Kerpchar
Gino Lazzari
Jeannie McBride
Dwight McKee
Edward Mokos
Nancy Monzi
Joseph Morace
Wasyl Polischuk
Gerald Rockey
Sharon Rockey
Albert Risdorfer
Mary M. Russell
Lois Ryals
Connie Schaffer
Luke Schultz
Diana Schwandt
Gregory Smith
Paul Spear
George Van Durick
Margaret Ward
Joan Weiner, Esq.
Michael Zaffiri

MAGLOCLEN
Brooke Appleby
Jean Degnan
Marilyn B. Peterson
Alexander J. Rock
Warren B. Surdam
Margaret Taylor

LEVITICUS
Julie Brinkley
Deborah Feurer
George Galovitch
Bill Richett

Acknowledgements

This report is the result of an intensive investigation and analysis done by the Southeastern Regional Office with the cooperation of numerous other agencies.

Staff members who participated in the investigation under the direction of Special Agent in Charge Frank Booth are:

Carl Brown
Vincent Clemente
Victor DiCicco
Jeannie McBride
Joseph Morace
Jack Murmylo
Albert Risdorfer
Gerald Rockey
Joseph Salerno
Carol Salter

John Contino, Esq. was the legal advisor to the investigation. Marilyn B. Peterson edited this document.

Special acknowledgements go to Gregory Magarity, Esq., who acted as Special Counsel to the Crime Commission for the public hearings held July 28, 29 and 30, 1981.

The following agencies and individuals were instrumental in aiding the Commission in its investigation:

Arizona Drug Control District, Tucson
California Department of Justice
Illinois Department of Law Enforcement
Illinois Legislative Investigating Commission
Long Beach, California, Police Department
Los Angeles, California, Police Department
New Jersey State Police
New York Department of Labor
New York Police Department
New York State Commission of Investigation
New York State Organized Crime Task Force
Pennsylvania State Police
Philadelphia Police Department
Phoenix, Arizona, Police Department
Riverside County Sheriff's Office, California
Department of Justice
United States Department of Justice Strike Force, Philadelphia and Los Angeles

The Commission

The Pennsylvania Crime Commission is an independent state agency mandated to investigate organized crime and public corruption, to issue reports on these investigations to the General Assembly and the people, and to refer information on criminal violations to prosecutors and other law enforcement agencies.

The Pennsylvania Crime Commission Act (Act of October 4, 1978, P. L. 876, No. 169) became effective on December 4, 1978. Prior laws and executive orders authorized the work of the Commission since 1967.

Due to the Commission's unique status, it can focus on broad or narrow patterns of organized criminal activity. Its purpose is not to look at isolated, transactional, incidents of criminal activity in one municipality or another. The Commission looks at patterns and interrelationships of criminal activities across the state, which extend beyond the geographic or capability range of existing police agencies.

The Commission maintains one headquarters and four regional offices in the state. It has a current authorized personnel complement of 57 positions. In addition, the Commission is the recipient of two federal grants with authorized personnel complements totalling 13 positions.

Those two grants fund the Leviticus and MAGLOCEN projects. Leviticus is a seven-state consortium of law enforcement and regulatory agencies which focuses on fraud in the coal industry. MAGLOCLEN is an association of more than a dozen major law enforcement agencies in eight states. It is designed to provide investigative and technical support, an information system, and auxilliary funding to aid those agencies in the apprehension of organized criminals involved in interstate activities.

Through its work with these projects and its ongoing investigations, the Pennsylvania Crime Commission continues working toward cooperative law enforcement activities in Pennsylvania. The realization of this goal will greatly enhance law enforcement's ability to fight organized crime.

Contents

Investigative Summary

This report is one result of a three-year investigation by the Pennsylvania Crime Commission into the influence of organized crime in the field of pre-paid health care services and the questionable business activities engaged in by some health care plan providers.

As examples of these situations in the health plan industry, the Commission looked into three companies: Labor Health Plans, Inc. (LHP), of Chicago; the A.M.M.A. Health Center, Inc., in Philadelphia; and American Health Programs, Inc., (AHP), located in Trevose, Bucks County.

The Commission's investigation found links between traditional organized criminals and two of the companies—Labor Health Plans and A.M.M.A. This report shows that La Cosa Nostra members or associates were instrumental in helping these companies receive union contracts. Moreover, there were indications that, in other cases, the unions were aware that La Cosa Nostra groups would reap financial benefits if the contracts were awarded to particular companies.

This association between some unions and traditional organized crime figures displays the influence over ranking union members which organized criminals sometimes have.

The investigation into American Health Programs (AHP) Inc. showed no links to traditional organized crime. The company did, however, seem to have contacts in the unions or with people close to the unions which increased the likelihood of their receiving the health plan contract. Often, these contacts were paid substantial fees or commissions for their efforts.

The Commission further investigated the two local companies, A.M.M.A. and AHP, to determine if there was any fraudulent activities in the administration of dental and health plans offered by these companies. In both cases, it was found that services rendered were substantially over-reported to the client unions and that the companies were involved in questionable investments.

In the case of A.M.M.A., the Commission obtained records from participating doctors and clinics. These reports showed that, in relation to a contract with Teamsters Local 837, A.M.M.A. over-reported the value of services received by union members by $254,715.

AHP had several large contracts with local unions including AFSCME District Council 33 and the Retail Clerks Union, Delaware Valley Health and Welfare Fund. The Commission obtained worksheets prepared by an AHP employee, Carol P. Lozanoff, which showed wide discrepancies between actual and reported usage of services of these two unions. In all, AHP reported over $2 million in value of services to the unions which were never received.

Through the falsification of utilization reports and the omission of actual profits made from the contracts, both companies were able to convince union leaders that their services were necessary and within a reasonable price range.

While the Commission was unable to determine the actual profits garnered by either company, there are some indications that the companies had money readily available for some questionable investments.

A.M.M.A., for example, was able to loan nearly $160,000 to companies which had close ties to its owners over a three-year period. In some cases, these loans were interest-free and were never repaid.

AHP used nearly $2.5 million for bonuses to top-level employees and loans and investments during a two-year period. A number of these investments have shown no appreciable return to date.

In summary, the Crime Commission found that the three health plan providers used questionable marketing techniques, did not provide their clients with actual accountings of their services or profits, and utilized those profits in an unsound business manner.

Conclusions

As a result of the Crime Commission's exhaustive investigation, the following conclusions have been reached:

1. Traditional and non traditional organized criminals have infiltrated pre-paid health and dental care plan organizations throughout the country. These organized criminals and their associates have diverted millions of dollars from union health and welfare trust funds through these organizations.

2. Various union health and welfare fund trustees and administrators have neglected their fiduciary responsibility in the award and administration of health care benefits. Such contracts are sometimes awarded on the basis of favoritism rather than cost-effectiveness. While the contracts are in force, the unions may neglect to require the health plan organizations to provide them with detailed accountings of services rendered, actual costs and profits made.

3. Some Pennsylvania-based pre-paid health care plan organizations have submitted misleading and deceptive reports to union health and welfare fund trustees regarding benefit utilization by union members. These reports have contained figures inflated to as much as 600 percent of actual and have resulted in contract renewals which might not have been given if the actual number of services had been reported.

4. Some pre-paid health care plan organizations have utilized questionable marketing techniques. Payments have been made to individuals who were in some way associated with the awarding of health care plan contracts. Substantial commissions and consulting fees have been paid to individuals in return for minimal services.

5. Pennsylvania-based health care plan organizations have been involved in financial transactions which reduced the financial soundness of the organization. Several of these transactions involved loans to or through individuals with close ties to the health care plan organizations.

6. Pennsylvania law does not regulate profit making pre-paid health care plan organizations. Loopholes in the current law encourage the types of questionable activities found in this report.

7. Municipalities in the Commonwealth have no authority over the award and administration of health care benefit contracts for public sector or municipal employees.

8. These findings are not unique to health care plan organizations in the Commonwealth. Similar activities have been uncovered in other jurisdictions.

Recommendations

A. The Professional Health Services Corporations Act in Pennsylvania should be amended to include the following provisions to regulate profit-making health care plan providers:

- the submission of clear and complete statements of benefit coverage
- limitations on the amount that these companies can spend on marketing and administration
- the filing of detailed annual reports
- the regulation of investments
- a certification of authority to transact business
- the disclosure of the identity of consultants to the company, particularly those used for marketing
- yearly audits and certification by a Certified Public Accountant
- that incorporators must be competent and trustworthy
- a strict conflict of interest provision

B. The Employee Retirement and Income Security Act (ERISA), should be amended to cover trustees and administrators of public employee health and welfare funds.

C. Municipalities should be allowed to audit health and welfare funds for which they provide funding and should be part of the benefit provider selection process.

D. The U.S. Department of Labor should conduct periodic and random audits of union health and welfare and pension funds.

E. Union members should have the ability to initiate a civil action to recover trust fund money that has been lost through either criminal or negligent conduct of the trust fund trustees or administrator.

F. In the case of public sector unions, the governmental unit that supplies the funds for the purchase of benefit programs should have the ability to initiate a civil action to recover health and welfare fund money that has been lost through criminal or negligent conduct by trust fund trustees or administrators.

G. The government should have the ability to recover on behalf of union trust funds, excess commissions or finder's fees.

H. Trustees and administrators should be liable for treble damages for losses resulting from their conduct.

Chapter One
A National Problem

A National Problem

The infiltration of organized crime into health care plan organizations has become a national problem. Fraud in the health care industry is on the increase and contributes to the skyrocketing costs of health services.

The Commission's investigation has documented links between organized crime and health care service providers through union contracts in over a half-dozen states. (See chart, page 00). Our findings, coupled with those of other state law enforcement agencies, reinforces the conclusion that this industry is under-regulated and, therefore, susceptible to fraudulent activity.

How Health Plans work

In 1979, the total cost of national health care was over $212 billion. This figure included the cost of personal health care, administration and prepayment expenses, government public health activities, research and construction. This computes to approximately $943 per person.

The cost of personal health care services represents 89 percent of total health care costs and includes $40.6 billion for physician services, $13.6 billion for dental services, $17 billion for prescription care, and $4.4 billion for vision care. Another $7.7 billion was expended in 1979 for prepayment and administrative expenses.* The costs are obviously staggering.

A large portion of personal health care costs are shouldered by the nation's employers in the form of employee health and welfare benefit packages. The National Center for Health Care Services Research recently reported that, in 1977, approximately 85 million American workers were covered by health insurance plans at work. The average annual premium per workers was reported to be $590, of which $501 was contributed by the employer.

All figures from the* ***Book of Health Insurance Data* *(1980-81) prepared for the Health Insurance Association of America by the Health Insurance Institute.*

For example, a dentist might receive $5 per month per patient or family as a fixed fee. This would compute to $60 per year per patient. If the patient only made one visit during that year, and received $30 worth of services, the dentist would make an additional $30. However, if the patient made five visits at $30 each (totalling $150), the dentist would 'lose' $90 in services for that year. However, there is ample opportunity, if the contract continues, to recoup this 'loss'.

More complex work is covered, in the fixed-fee method, by a combination of basic fees received plus patient payments.

The cost of these benefits are generally passed on to the consumer in the form of increasing product costs. In the case of public employee unions, health and welfare benefits costs are borne by the taxpayer.

The employer generally, through collective bargaining agreements, contributes an agreed upon amount of money into a trust or health and welfare fund for the purchase of health care benefits on behalf of labor organization or trade union members. In the case of a union which represents municipal or government personnel, the funds are supplied by the municipality or state.

A board of trustees then seeks applications from providers of health care benefits. Those applications are reviewed and the provider is then selected. It should be noted that the provider who contracts with the union is most often not the end provider of health care. Rather, it is an administrative company which handles the medical and/or dental claims.

Many health care benefit packages are provided by established insurance companies. Others are provided by non-profit health plan organization or profit-oriented health plan organizations. The types of companies dealt with in this report are profit making health plan organizations.

There are two ways that these benefit package plans can work. In one case, the health care plan company establishes what the usual and customary charge is for various specific services. The employee or union member may visit the doctor or dentist of their choice, but the health plan organization only pays this customary fee and any amount over that must be borne by the patient.

Under the second method, the health plan organization enlists participating doctors or dentists in a geographic area and receives an agreement with these participating specialists to accept a fixed fee per patient. This fee is paid monthly by the health plan organization and is received by participating physicians and dentists regardless of how many (or how few) visits are made by the patient.

The Roles Of Organized Crime

The Crime Commission's *1980 Report*, which looked at criminal activities during the 1970s, defined organized crime as groups of people working together, usually on an ongoing basis, in a mix of legal and illegal activities. It further noted that one goal of organized crime is to achieve monopolistic control over certain industries or commercial ventures to further their economic gain.

The public and some law enforcement agencies view organized crime as synonymous with La Cosa Nostra. This misconception is one which denies the mounting evidence of criminal groups with varied ethnicities and common, illegal, goals.

The Commission's investigation into health care plans documents involvement in these plans by members and associates of La Cosa Nostra. However, in the section on American Health Programs, Inc., it also shows the involvement of business and professional people who conspired on a continuing basis to conduct their business in a fraudulent manner.

Interestingly, the methods employed by these dissimilar groups of organized criminals appear to be quite similar.

The examples within this report show the relationship between traditional organized crime and the health care plan industry. In the section on Labor Health Plans, Inc., La Cosa Nostra members and associates are used as intermediaries to help the company obtain contracts. A similar situation seemed to be in evidence with A.M.M.A. Health Center, Inc.

During the Commission's public hearings on July 28, 1981, former Cosa Nostra member Aladena "Jimmy the Weasel" Fratianno testified about the role which he and others played in regard to health care plan contracts in other states:

Q: And the insurance and the health plans is a new avenue of making money for the families, is it not?
Fratianno **(A):** They've been doing that quite a while.
Q: Quite a while?
A: Yes, they have.
Q: Now, how does it work exactly? Why is it important for the people who are participating in this to use a La Cosa Nostra member? How does that help them?
A: They have connections.
Q: How?
A: Well, they know that they have an idea of who they are. They know that they can get things done.
Q: It's mainly through the connections? Or is it also through the threats or implied threats of having a family member involved?
A: That goes along with it; a little fear, you know.
Q: A little fear doesn't hurt in persuading somebody to contract; is that it?
A: That's correct.
Q: And if the fear doesn't work, they might use actual force; is that correct?
A: It's very possible. It's been done.
Q: . . . the connections that you've described are through certain labor leaders, certain people who control or have access to the administration of these funds, correct?
A: That's correct, sir.
Q: Like you described (Jack) Presser* and the other people such as that.
A: (Witness nodded).
Q: And this enables them to take over the funds and use them for their own advantage. Do they have any competition really?
A: Oh, there's a lot of people trying to get these programs, sir. Whoever's got the best connection gets, gets the contract.
Q: So the competition is usually of the illegal variety, isn't it?
A: I would say so, yes.
Q: And by getting the contracts, they then inflate the prices, correct?
A: Well, no. They don't inflate the prices. It's so lucrative that you don't have to inflate; due to inflation, they go up anyhow. Every year they go up. The wages go up, the benefits go up, it goes up anyhow.

But it's so lucrative that you actually don't have to, to raise the prices too much.

Fratianno, who acted as a contract for Angelo Commito and Labor Health Plans, Inc., testified later that, "I was promised ten thousand a month, if I got that program, for myself."

**Presser is the vice president of the International Brotherhood of Teamsters.*

From the health care plan provider's point of view, the Cosa Nostra members were acting as contacts with the unions. Fratianno also explained why the Cosa Nostra could act in this role:

A: So he (Jack Presser) has an obligation. And he knows that without them people he wouldn't last two minutes in the Teamsters Union.
Q: Did you have a conversation with Mr. Presser concerning Angelo Commito?
A: Yes, sir.
Q: Would you please relate the circumstances of the conversation you had with Mr. Presser concerning Angelo Commito?
A: Well, I had some other business with Jackie Presser. In the same conversation I told him that Commito was—we were doing business with Commito, and that if he could help him in any way, it would mean money for us.
Q: What was Mr. Presser's response?
A: He said he would (do) what he can for him.
Q: Do you know whether Mr. Presser was aware of Commito's involvement with Jack Licavoli,** also known as Jack White, and Angelo Felice?
A: Well, he knew that whatever I did, the Cleveland Family would get a percentage of. So it actually didn't matter.

In the example which had no known organized crime ties, American Health Programs, Inc., other marketing agents were used. As is described in Chapter 4, the Commission received evidence that several people involved in unions or closely connected to the unions received monetary or other benefits for helping the company get health care contracts with the unions.

Those individuals included a union officer, a union trust fund trustee and an attorney. Like the Cosa Nostra members in the Labor Health Plans example, they were in a position to exert some control over the union's decision.

***Licavoli is the head of the Cleveland La Cosa Nostra family.*

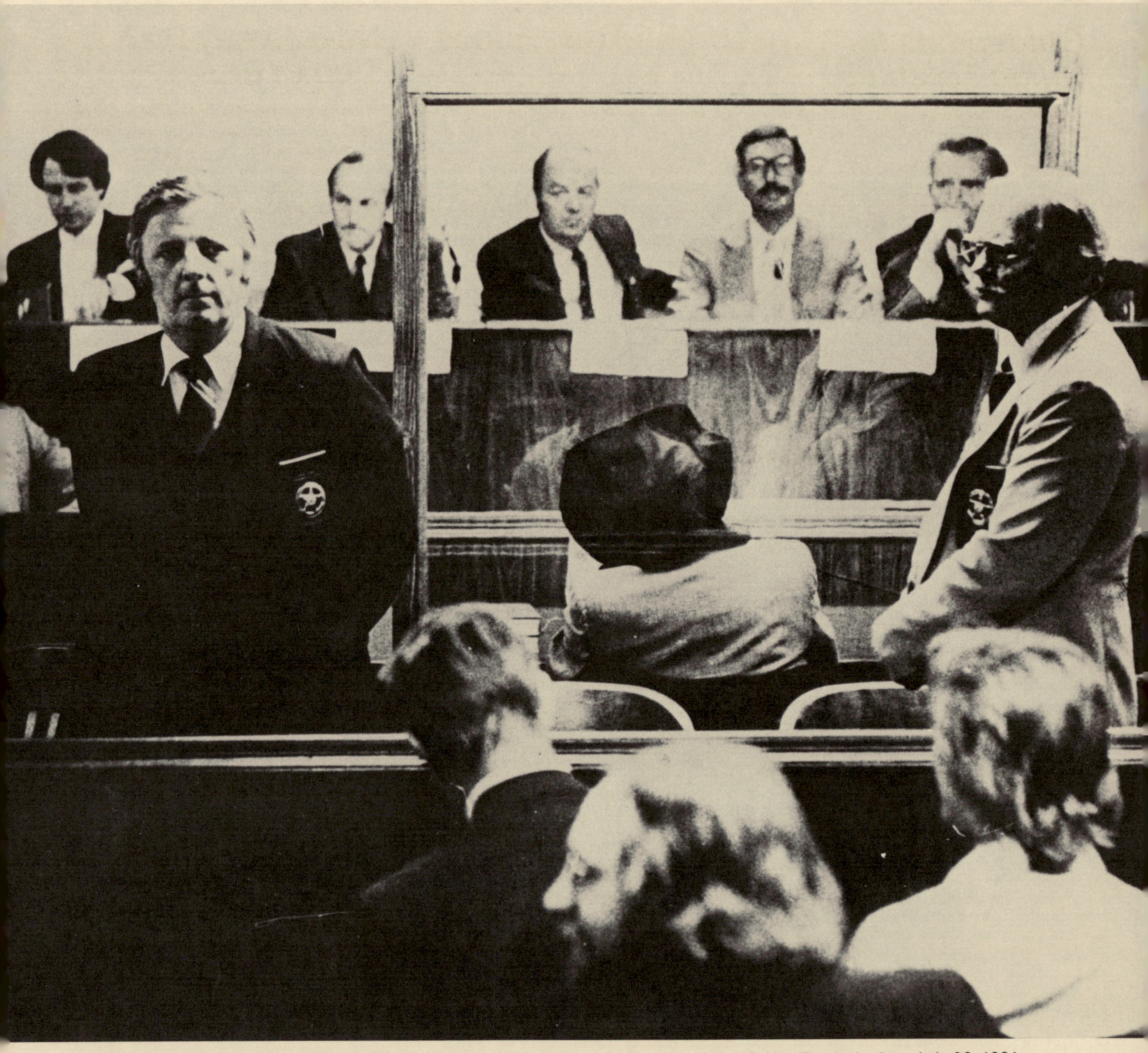

Aladena "Jimmy the Weasel" (hooded figure) testifying before the Pennsylvania Crime Commission, July 28, 1981.

It could be argued that these questionable marketing techniques are not dissimilar to those used in the business world on a daily basis. Choosing to do business with someone known rather than someone unknown is not a crime. Fratianno claimed that the union officials with whom he dealt were aware that their acceptance of the health plan would be financially rewarding to Fratianno and were agreeable to that.

Non-traditional organized crime activity was further found in the daily operations of American Health Programs, Inc. and the A.M.M.A. Health Center, Inc. Chapters 3 and 4 detail the way in which both companies provided their unions with inflated reports on usage of their services, and, in essence, deceived the union about what its employees were receiving in return for the health care premiums.

It can be seen, therefore, that both traditional and non-traditional organized crime figures are heavily involved in at least some health care plan companies, and that their involvement is for the purpose of their personal financial gain. It is the belief of the Commission and other law enforcement officials that the companies in this report are indicative of similar operations in health care companies across the nation.

Guideposts for Union Trustees

In order to ensure the most effective operation of a trust fund and avoid breaches of fiduciary responsibility, trustees and administrators should employ basic precautions in their general activities. The trustees should:

- be aware of their civil and criminal liabilities under the ERISA law.
- employ an independent consultant to analyse and evaluate the competitive bids submitted by potential benefit plan providers.
- ascertain to whom brokers' fees or commissions have been paid in relation to the award of a benefits package.
- employ a financial consultant to review the health plan provider's financial and utilization records during the life of the contract.
- require in-depth periodic reports by the benefit plan provider which should include figures relating to utilization by the eligible members, services received, an itemized cost of administration and the amount of trust fund monies actually spent to provide the benefits to union members.

Union Trust Funds

The key ingredient in the provision of health care services is the recipient of those services, the union or employee group member. It is on their behalf, and ostensibly for their benefit, that these contracts are entered into.

Generally, it is the union's officials or trust fund trustees who make the decision on who will provide the union with health care services. As was mentioned in the previous section and is detailed in later chapters, the Commission found that some union officials allegedly received financial remuneration for their acquiescence to certain contract proposals.

Labor racketeering and the infiltration of organized crime into union trust funds has been described as the nation's number one investigative priority by many law enforcement authorities. It has been documented that once in control of that trust fund or the organization that is to provide health care benefits for the union members, organized crime figures have been able to drain millions of dollars from the fund.

Marty Steinberg, Chief Counsel for the United States Senate Permanent Sub-Committee on Investigations, testified before the Pennsylvania Crime Commission and described the methods employed by organized crime figures to fraudulently deplete union health and welfare trust funds.

These methods include multiple billings to the trust fund by the health care provider, false or fraudulent loans from the trust fund to outside parties, inflated service contracts, kickbacks to union or trust fund officials, unnecessary or inflated commissions relating to health care benefit contracts and questionable investments.

In addition, Steinberg testified that the health care provider or insurer often billed the trust fund for services that were never supplied or reported an inflated number of services.

Instances such as those described by Steinberg were found to occur in several local health plan contracts. The union's role in some instances was possibly a complicit one. In other cases, the union was allegedly unaware of the health plan company's activities.

A question remains, however, of the unions' responsibility to their members to demand accurate reporting of service usage from the health plan provider.

New Jersey Plan Tied to Bruno

In December 1980, the New Jersey State Commission of Investigation conducted public hearings and later issued a public report detailing organized crime infiltration of New Jersey dental care plans.

The New Jersey report revealed that North American Dental Plans, Inc., a Wayne, Pennsylvania, corporation, had hired a consulting firm, Rittenhouse Consulting Enterprises, Ltd. of Cherry Hill, New Jersey, run by Lawrence A. Smith, to secure a prepaid dental benefit contract with Local 170 of the Hotel and Restaurant Employees Union in Camden, New Jersey.* The union, which later became known as Local 33, was run by Ralph Natale and Albert Daidone, the vice-president of the local.**

The New Jersey investigation revealed that Rittenhouse had received substantial monies from N.A.D.P. in return for obtaining the contract, although other work was supposed to be provided. The investigation also revealed that the trustees of the health and welfare fund of the union made little or no determination as to which plan was to be chosen; rather they relied upon the advice of one or two individuals who were connected with organized crime.

**NADP is run by Joseph R. Cusumano of Devon, Pennsylvania. The company is a subsidiary of Health Corporation of America, also located in Wayne, Pennsylvania. For more on NADP and HCA see page 29.*

***Ralph Natale is a close associate of many organized crime figures and has been described by organized crime hitman Charles Allen as a member of the Philadelphia crime family. Natale is currenting serving a 12-year prison term for his role in the arson of the Mr. Livingroom Furniture Store in Marlton, NJ. Natale was also convicted in July 1980 of smuggling cocaine into the United States.*

Further investigation revealed that Smith could not account for approximately $150,000 of the $800,000 Rittenhouse had received in 1978. According to the New Jersey Commission, this cash was funneled to Angelo Bruno, deceased Philadelphia crime boss, through Natale and Philadelphia organized crime figure Raymond "Long John" Martorano.*

The influence of organized crime in the selection of union health care providers was amply portrayed in the New Jersey investigation through confessed Mafia hit-man Charles Allen, who testified before the New Jersey Commission. Allen testified that "Ralph Natale had it all set up for, for his cousin to run the dental plan, but he was called to Philadelphia by Angelo Bruno." Allen further testified that "Angelo told him, 'No, Ralph, your cousin's not going to have the dental plan, Larry Smith is going to have it.' "

The New Jersey State Commission of Investigation also focused on a North New Jersey dental plan called Joel S. Sokol, D.D.S., P. A. The investigation illustrated that the plan utilized out of state organized crime connected advance men in its creation and employed Comillo Molinaro, an admitted organized crime member, on its premises as a janitor to look after the interests of John Riggi.

Riggi has been described as the individual in charge of Simone (Sam) DeCavalcante's New Jersey organized crime family. Riggi had been involved in the Sokol program contract awards.

In addition, the investigation revealed that the Sokol plan provided free service to organized crime members and associates, inflated invoices for equipment and fixtures prior to transferring the overage into cash, and further drained cash from the operation through inflated construction invoices and fictitious vendors and payees.**

For more information regarding Martorano's involvement in the health care industry see page 20.

***New Jersey reported that the Sokol Plan had connections with John (Curly) Montana, identified by New Jersey authorities as a Cleveland organized crime figure, and Carl Rizzo, identified by New Jersey authorities as an organized crime figure from Buffalo, New York. Rizzo was found garroted in the trunk of a car in April 1980. For more on Rizzo's connection to the PCC investigation see page 18.*

Fraud in New York

In March 1981, the State Commission of Investigation in New York issued a public report entitled "A Trust Betrayed: Fraud, Breach of Fiduciary Duty and Waste at the Teamsters Local 237 Welfare Fund." The report outlined the various transactions regarding Teamsters Local 237, a union representing over 14,000 New York City employees.*

In 1967, Barry Feinstein became president of the union and chairman of the fund's board of trustees. As chairman of the board of trustees, Feinstein selected William Wallach, a longtime friend and relative by marriage, as the fund's insurance broker and consultant.

Together with Calvin Winick, another insurance broker, Wallach defrauded the fund of over $3 million from 1972 through 1980. The Commission concluded that this could not have happened if the trustees of the fund had properly exercised their fiduciary obligations to preserve the fund's assets.

The investigation focused on how Wallach and Winick defrauded the fund by obtaining illegal commissions from the fund's insurer, Trans World Life Insurance Company of New York, in return for placing the fund's business with Trans World. These commissions, which were concealed from the fund, were passed on as premium charges to the fund.

The investigation further revealed the efforts Feinstein made to assure that Wallach and Winick would continue to receive exorbitant payments even after he knew of their fraud, including his efforts to influence the progress of an audit by the New York City Comptroller's office and a later investigation by the New York State Insurance Department.

The report also detailed the failure of those entrusted with the preservation of the fund's assets, including Feinstein, the trustees, and the fund's counsel, to prevent the fund from being victimized. The New York Commission concluded that the approximately $140 million in health and welfare funds provided by the city of New York are almost entirely unregulated.

This local is the largest Teamster's public employee union in the nation.

As a result of the joint efforts by New York authorities, the New York State Insurance Department in April 1980, was able to recover $1.3 million from Trans World in relation to the commission paid for the Local 237 health and welfare benefits.

In yet another situation, the New York State Insurance Department was able to recover an additional $345,426 of allegedly improper service fees that had been paid to the Connecticut General Life Insurance Company.

These fees had been paid in relation to health and welfare benefits for the Operating Engineers Local 138, Farmingdale, New York; Teamsters Local 282, Elmont, New York; and the Amalgamated Transit Union Local 1181, Ozone Park, New York.

The State Insurance Department contended that these fees had been improper because they should not have been paid, were for minimal work, or were for services duplicating those done by the insurance company of the welfare fund employees.

Federal Investigations

While the federal investigations of this area are too numerous to list or detail, several substantive cases of corrupt and questionable activity have been documented throughout the country and should be mentioned.

In 1979, the Committee on Government Affairs of the United States Senate, Permanent Sub-Committee on Investigations, issued a report of its investigation into the labor union insurance activities of Joseph Hauser and his associates.

According to the Sub-Committee's report, Hauser carried out a massive insurance sales scheme targeted at union health and welfare trust funds in Florida, Indiana, Massachusetts, Arizona and the Teamsters Central States, Southwest and Southeast area health and welfare funds.* Hauser and his associates had acquired the business from the labor union trust funds generally through the influence of persons close to the unions.

Hauser controlled the Farmers National Life Insurance Company, a small financially troubled Florida insurance company and a subsidiary of Farmers in Arizona, Family Provider Life Insurance Company.

The Sub-Committee's investigation concluded that of approximately $39 million in union insurance premiums obtained by Hauser's companies, $11 million was diverted to other firms in the form of questionable commissions and commission advances, worthless and questionable investments, conversions to cash and the payment of personal expenses and legal fees.

Hauser, who operated with Bernard Rubin, President of the Southeast Florida laborer's unions in Miami, Florida, was convicted in 1977 for his activity in attempting to bribe union officials to do business with his firm, National Prepaid Health Plans in California.

In 1979, Hauser also pleaded guilty to federal charges in Arizona for related activities. Rubin pleaded guilty in December 1978 for his involvement with Hauser in Arizona.

In a related matter which further documents organized crime infiltration into this area, a federal grand jury in Florida on June 4, 1981, indicted 14 men on charges of violating the Federal Racketeer Influenced and Corrupt Organization Act (RICO). Among the individuals indicted were the boss of the Tampa, Florida based organized crime family Santo Trafficante and the boss of the Chicago organized crime family Anthony "Big Tuna" Accardo. Joseph Hauser was named in the indictment as an unindicted co-conspirator.

The indictment charged that the principals had established a scheme whereby insurance companies would be established or expanded to obtain the pension, health, vision and dental policies of the Laborer's International Union of North America which represents 75,000 workers. The companies would then kickback part of the profits to the principals. The indictment alleged that as part of the scheme, a land development company was established through which the funds would be laundered. Seven union officials were also indicted.

While the above instances are but a few of the situations that have been experienced with relation to organized crime's infiltration and the corruption of union health and welfare funds and the health care providers administration and insurers, they serve to document the prevalence of such activity throughout the nation and further display the complex nature of such activity. The types of activity described in these cases will continue to grow, as this area continues to offer lucrative opportunities for unscrupulous individuals.

Current Laws

A significant aspect of the Crime Commission's investigation showed that profit-making health care plan organizations are not subject to any general regulatory authority in the Commonwealth of Pennsylvania. In addition, the fiduciary responsibilities placed on union trust fund officials by the federal Employee Retirement Income Security Act (ERISA) is not applicable to public sector union officials. These loopholes in the law allow health care plan organizations to act in the manner uncovered by the Commission in this report.

Pennsylvania Law

Profit-making health care plan companies are not covered under any Pennsylvania law, but similar types of companies that offer comparable benefits are regulated. For example, insurance companies which offer prepaid health care benefits to union groups are subject to state insurance laws.

In addition, non-profit corporations that offer health, dental, optometric, or other medical service plans are regulated under the Professional Health Services Plan Corporations Act. Nonprofit companies fall under the guidance of the Pennsylvania Departments of Health and Insurance.*

The Professional Health Services Plan Corporations Act (40 p. s., 6301 *et seq.*) was enacted to provide adequate health services to low-income persons.

This law requires the issuance of a Certificate of Authority to the nonprofit company after its approval by the Pennsylvania Department of Health. It requires an initial financial reserve and a continuing reserve fund which ensures service to enrolled subscribers.

It further requires approval by the Department of Health of the company's rates, the form and content of contracts, methods and rates of payment to participating doctors, acquisition costs in procuring subscribers and the depletion of the company's reserves by more than 20 percent in any one year. In addition, it requires the filing of annual reports and regulates, generally, the investment of funds by the non-profit companies.

The law contains criminal penalties of a $3,000 fine or six months imprisonment for violations of the Act.

Several of its provisions, however, are unique to its stated purpose of providing health services to low-income persons.

For example, the non-profit entities are exempt from state tax laws and must set standards for the provision of health care services to low income people. If, as the Commission recommends, (see page 2) amendments to this law are proposed, a careful analysis of which provisions would be applicable to profit-making companies would have to be made.

Pennsylvania law also regulates health maintenance organizations, under the Pennsylvania Health Maintenance Organization Act. This act only applies to entities that provide a full spectrum of basic health care services, and was amended in 1980 to include profit-making entities.

Other States

At the present time, thirteen states have enacted comprehensive controls for fixed-fee dental and profit making health care plan organizations. States with such legislation include Arizona, California, Colorado, Connecticut, Florida, Indiana, Nevada, New Jersey, New Mexico, South Carolina, Texas, Virginia and Washington. As of June, 1981, legislation was pending in Nebraska, Ohio and Utah. (See charts, pages 00 and 00, for types of legislation covering health care industry in these and other states.)

Generally, health care plan legislation requires a certificate of authority to transact business as a health or dental care plan entity and certain filings must be made to obtain such certificates. These laws also have solvency provisions requiring the submission of a fidelity bond in specified amounts on behalf of each officer responsible for conducting corporate affairs. In addition, a number of states require the maintenance of a surety bond or corporate reserve fund guaranteeing services under the plan.

Another feature of the legislation in four states is a decreasing limitation on the amount of funds that may be used for marketing, administration and solicitation.

* *On October 30, 1981, the Pennsylvania Department of Insurance issued an opinion that profit-making health plan providers are not subject to current insurance laws and are not within the jurisdiction of the Department.*

LEGISLATIVE ENACTMENTS OF SELECTED STATES

STATE / PLANS REGULATED	ARIZONA DENTAL	COLORADO DENTAL	NEW MEXICO DENTAL	NEW JERSEY DENTAL	INDIANA HEALTH CARE	WASHINGTON HEALTH CARE	VIRGINIA HEALTH CARE	TEXAS HEALTH CARE
(A) REQUIRED FILINGS FOR CERTIFICATE OF AUTHORITY								
Financial Statement	▒	▒	▒	▒			▒	▒
Independent Certified Audit				█				
Proposed Provider Contract	▒	▒	▒	▒		▒	▒	▒
Proposed Form of Membership Coverage	▒	▒	▒	▒	▒	▒	▒	▒
Plan Description	▒	▒	▒	▒	▒	▒	▒	▒
Officer Identification	▒	▒	▒	▒	▒	▒	▒	▒
Organizational Documents	▒	▒	▒	▒	▒	▒	▒	▒
Description of Proposed Method of Marketing	▒	▒	▒	▒	▒		▒	▒
Source of Working Capital	▒	▒	▒	▒	▒		▒	▒
Evidence of Quality Assurance Program			▒	▒			▒	▒
Cost Accounting Program				▒				
Evidence of Complaint Review System				▒			▒	▒
Officer Conflict of Interest Disclosure							▒	
(B) ISSUANCE OF CERTIFICATE OF AUTHORITY (Following Conditions Must Be Satisfied)								
Corporate Officer Integrity	▒		▒	▒	▒	▒	▒	▒
Career Offender Cartel Provision				█				
Financial Responsibility	▒	▒	▒	▒	▒		▒	▒
Alternative Coverage Provision	▒		▒	▒	▒		▒	▒
Sufficiency of Providers Agreement	▒	▒	▒	▒	▒		▒	
Satisfactory Rate Schedule	▒		▒	▒	▒		▒	
(C) SURETY OR FIDELITY BOND								
Corporate Bond Based on Enrolled Members	▒	▒	▒					
Officer Bond—$50,000	▒	▒	▒					
Officer Bond Set By Insurance Department				▒				
Corporate Bond, 2.5% of Gross Annual Fees or 250,000					▒			
Bond Amount Set By Insurance Department						▒	▒	▒
(D) CORPORATE RESERVE FUND								
2% of Annual Net Prepayments								
Up to $500,000	▒	▒	▒					
Up to $100,000				▒				
Amount Set By Insurance Department						▒		
(E) CORPORATE TAX								
1% of Annual Net Prepayments on Domestic Plans	▒	▒	▒					
2% of Annual Net Prepayments on Foreign Plan	▒	▒	▒					
Other								▒
(F) REGULATION OF OPERATIONAL EXPENSES								
Expenditures Limited To:								
30% of Prepaid Charges in First Year	▒	▒	▒	▒				
25% of Prepaid Charges in Second Year	▒	▒	▒	▒				
20% of Prepaid Charges Thereafter	▒	▒	▒	▒				
For: Administration	▒	▒	▒					
Marketing	▒	▒	▒					
Solicitation	▒	▒	▒					
General Expenses				▒				
Acquisitions				▒				
Taxes and Licenses				▒				
(G) ANNUAL REPORTING REQUIREMENTS								
Financial Statement	▒	▒	▒	▒	▒	▒	▒	▒
Modification From Prior Reports	▒	▒	▒	▒			▒	▒
Number of New Members	▒	▒	▒	▒	▒		▒	▒
Number of Members Terminated		▒	▒	▒	▒		▒	▒
Total Members					▒			
Cost of Care Provided	▒		▒					
Units of Care Provided	▒		▒					
Operation Costs		▒						
Pattern of Service Utilization		▒					▒	
Complaints Received				▒			▒	
Malpractice Experience				▒			▒	
Certified Audit				▒				
Annual Report, Public Document				▒	▒			▒
Source of Funds				█				
Disposition of Funds				█				
Financial Report Enrollees					▒			▒
Other Report for Enrollees								▒

▒ Statutory Provisions

█ Proposed Amendments by State Commission of Investigation

LEGISLATIVE ENACTMENTS OF SELECTED STATES continued

STATE	ARIZONA	COLORADO	NEW MEXICO	NEW JERSEY	INDIANA	WASHINGTON	VIRGINIA	TEXAS
PLANS REGULATED	DENTAL	DENTAL	DENTAL	DENTAL	HEALTH CARE	HEALTH CARE	HEALTH CARE	HEALTH CARE
(H) REGULATION OF AGENTS								
License Required	▓		▓		▓	▓	▓	▓
Disciplinary Provisions	▓		▓					
Regulation of Broker or Finder Fees				█				
Consultant Regulation and Reporting Requirements				█				
Malpractice Coverage for Providers				▓				
(I) MEMBERSHIP COVERAGE PROVISIONS								
Must Issue Evidence of Coverage	▓	▓	▓	▓	▓		▓	▓
Newborn Child Coverage Provision	▓	▓	▓			▓		
Description of Plan Benefits	▓	▓	▓	▓	▓		▓	▓
Description of Plan Limitations	▓	▓	▓	▓	▓		▓	▓
Identification of Information Services	▓	▓	▓	▓	▓		▓	▓
Member Payment Obligations	▓	▓	▓	▓	▓		▓	▓
Evidence of Coverage Must Be Approved	▓	▓	▓	▓	▓		▓	▓
Description of Complaint System				▓			▓	▓
(J) ADVERTISING AND SOLICITATION REGULATION								
Approval of Advertising Material	▓	▓	▓					
Unfair Trade and Fraud Provisions	▓	▓	▓	▓	▓	▓	▓	▓
Regulation of Corporate Name				▓		▓	▓	▓
Ethical Requirement for Sales Promotion	▓		▓					
Prohibition on Provider Evaluation	▓		▓					
(K) PERIODIC PLAN EXAMINATION BY STATE								
Review of:								
Financial Status	▓	▓	▓		▓			▓
Conduct of Business	▓	▓	▓		▓		▓	
Delivery of Care	▓	▓	▓				▓	
Complaint System				▓			▓	▓
Compliance With Recordkeeping Provisions				▓				
Compliance With Laws	▓	▓	▓	▓	▓			▓
General Examination				▓				
(L) MISCELLANEOUS PROVISIONS								
Regulation of Loans by a Plan				█			▓	▓
Authority to Promulgate Regulations	▓	▓	▓	▓	▓	▓	▓	▓
Liquidation Provisions	▓	▓	▓	▓			▓	▓
Regulation of Investments by a Plan					▓		▓	
Cancellation of Coverage Provisions					▓		▓	▓
Anti-Discrimination Provisions						▓	▓	
Illegal Rebate Provisions						▓		
Employee Payment Assumption Provision						▓		
Underwriting Requirements						▓		
Open Enrollment Provision and Exceptions							▓	
Officer Fiduciary Responsibility Provision							▓	▓
Out of Area Service Provision							▓	
(M) PENALTIES								
Revocation of Certificate of Authority	▓	▓	▓	▓	▓	▓	▓	▓
Suspension of Certificate of Authority	▓	▓	▓	▓	▓	▓	▓	▓
Cease and Desist Order		▓		▓		▓	▓	
Criminal Penalty				█		▓		▓
Civil Fine $100 to $500		▓				▓		
$500 to $1,000				▓				
$10,000				█				

▓ Statutory Provisions

█ Proposed Amendments by State Commission of Investigation

Under almost every statute, the health care plan organization must issue a clear and complete statement of benefit coverage, furnishing to every enrolled member the plan description, benefits available, limitations on service, co-payment responsibilities, and deductibles. It must also state where and in what manner information regarding the benefit program is available.

Health care plan organizations controlled by these laws must also file detailed annual reports, including financial statements and utilization information. Other provisions included in the laws provide for the licensing of brokers and agents, approval of advertising material, regulation of investments, and civil and criminal penalties for violations of the law.

In addition to the above provisions, the New Jersey State Commission of Investigation has recently recommended amendments to the New Jersey law. Included in these recommendations are provisions that would require the financial statement filed by the organization to be audited and certified by a Certified Public Accountant. Also, it would require regulation of and disclosures by all consultants to the organization and the regulation of broker or finders fee paid to such individuals. Also regulated would be loans made by health plan organizations.

While these provisions do not constitute the full range of considerations in the development and regulation of prepaid health care plan organizations, they do reflect some of the common concerns in other states.

ERISA and Other Controls

The federal Employee Retirement Income Security Act (ERISA) does not cover public sector union health and welfare trust funds, but most other union groups are guided by the restrictions in this law.

Generally, ERISA places strict fiduciary responsibility on health and welfare fund trustees and on the administrators of such funds. A breach of this responsibility, either through neglect or intention, may result in either civil or criminal liability. As is noted on page 00, the Commission recommends that ERISA be amended to cover public sector unions.

Pennsylvania has two laws which relate to public sector unions, but neither have provisions similar to ERISA. In addition, many municipalities in Pennsylvania have no power or authority over health and welfare benefits provided to public employees even though they provide the funds to cover the costs of those benefits.

In Philadelphia, the City has been able to obtain some representation and review authority over contracts for the provision of benefits by including the provisions for such authority in the collective bargaining agreements. In addition, the City is currently attempting to pass an ordinance that would give the City certain authority in relation to the expenditure of city funds for health and welfare benefits.

However, municipalities may be preempted from enacting laws governing to public sector health and welfare funds by virtue of the fact that there are two state statutes governing public union labor relations.

The Commission's Investigation

The investigation by the Pennsylvania Crime Commission into the medical and dental plan industry was, by far, the most complex investigation the Commission has done to date.

The initial resolution to open the investigation was passed by the Commissioners in the spring of 1978. When the Commission was reformed in 1979, another resolution continued the investigation. A total of two and a half years was spent on the investigation.

The financial complexity of the case required substantial and lengthy fiscal analyses by Special Agents who are Certified Public Accountants. The magnitude of the case required the close cooperation with a multitude of other law enforcement agencies.

This investigation required a total of 128 subpoenas to be served. Seventy-one were for public or private testimony, while 57 subpoenas were given to banks, corporations or other entities for records.

Of the persons who were subpoenaed to testify, 29 asserted their constitutional right against self-incrimination. Immunity was later granted to the following four persons:

Carol Lozanoff	(AHP)
Libby Barland	(AHP)
Sanford Roth	(AHP)
Roseann DiGrazio	(AMMA)

Sixteen litigations were entered into during the investigation, for the primary reason of enforcing subpoenas. Those who fought the Commission's subpoenas and the length of the court cases follow:

Robert Fleuhr (AMARC)	—4 months
Robert Rovner	—3 months
Howard Davidson	—4 months
Thomas Garvey	—5 months
Merrill Glickstein	—6 months

Alan Cohen and James Cox fought their subpoenas in court for less than a month.

During the course of this investigation, allegations of criminal or civil wrongdoing were forwarded to the United States Attorney (Philadelphia), the United States Strike Force (Philadelphia), the District Attorney (Philadelphia) and the Internal Revenue Service.

As a culmination to the investigation, the Commission held public hearings in Philadelphia on July 28, 29 and 30. Testimony was received from Commission personnel, law enforcement officers from other jurisdictions, and persons involved with the three companies being investigated. A significant witness at those hearings was Aladena "Jimmy the Weasel" Fratianno. His appearance and security were arranged through the cooperation of the United States Strike Force in Los Angeles, California, the United States Marshall's Service, and the Pennsylvania State Police.

In addition, testimony has been requested and given by Crime Commission personnel before the Pennsylvania House Committee on Consumer Affairs (September 9, 1981), and the United States House of Representatives Select Committee on Aging (November 4, 1981).

Chapter Two
Labor Health Plans, Inc.

Labor Health Plans, Inc.: From Chicago to the Coasts

Labor Health Plans, Inc., of 230 North Michigan Avenue in Chicago, came to the attention of the Crime Commission when its owner, Angelo T. Commito, began an attempt to market his plan in the Philadelphia area. A further investigation of Commito and his company showed a pattern of activity which had been repeated in locations from coast to coast.

Commito's usual procedure for gaining health contracts in various states was to first make contact with the local organized crime family. In the world of La Cosa Nostra, this contact is necessary protocol for anyone who wishes to do business in another family's territory.

Moreover, these contacts can help the potential health plan provider to find sources of financing for his local effort (as Commito attempted in Philadelphia), or they can provide him with introductions to local union leaders (as Commito found in Arizona and Ohio).

The following sections illustrate these contacts and their value to the health plan company.

A Local Sales Pitch

Labor Health Plans, Inc. is a Chicago-based corporation which administers medical and dental programs for unions. It is operated by Angelo T. Commito, who has residences in Chicago, Illinois and Sausalito, California.

During an attempt to market those services locally, Commito was observed meeting on several occasions with high-level organized crime figures in the Philadelphia area.*

Commito's first observed local contact took place on July 24, 1980. During a routine surveillance, special agents saw several men leaving the home of Frank "Frankie Flowers" D'Alfonso, a significant Philadelphia organized crime figure. (See D'Alfonso summary, page 16.)

**For information on Commito's midwest and west coast organized crime connections, see pages 17 to 19. Commito has twice been convicted on Internal Revenue Service violations in Illinois and Ohio. The Ohio conviction was related to a dental plan he provided in Columbus.*

These men were accompanied by D'Alfonso and drove to Philadelphia International Airport where one, later identified as Angelo T. Commito, boarded a Chicago-bound flight. A picture of Commito obtained during this surveillance is on page 00.

In November of 1980, a man named John James Allu* met with D'Alfonso and Mario Riccobene at Riccobene's residence. Allu, of New York, is an associate of the Genovese Cosa Nostra family. He is a former Teamsters Union official.**

John J. Allu

When the Commission checked the registration of the car driven to Philadelphia by Allu, it found that the car was registered to Labor Health Plans, Inc., Commito's company. Moreover, it learned that the registration for Labor Health Plans in New York is 12-29 31st Avenue, which is Allu's address and the address of a James Calandrillo, identified as a Gambino family member.

Mario Riccobene is a close associate of Philadelphia organized crime figures including his half-brother, Harry "Hunchback" Riccobene, who is a member of the Bruno/Testa/? crime family. In February of 1981, both of the Riccobenes were indicted by a federal grand jury in Philadelphia for their alleged roles in an illegal gambling operation which purportedly was in existence from 1972 to 1981.

While in Philadelphia, Allu was introduced by D'Alfonso to Nathan Steven Montrose, an insurance broker.

Montrose later introduced accountant Alan Cohen to Commito. Cohen was purportedly going to help get financing for the venture.

During January of 1981, D'Alfonso flew to Palm Springs, California and was observed in a meeting by California enforcement officials. Two of the individuals attending that meeting fit the descriptions of Commito and Allu. Furthermore, one of the vehicles used by these individuals was registered to an address used by Commito.

Also attending this Palm Springs meeting was a man identified as Frank Pries, also known as Frank Gulmi. New York authorities identify Pries as an administrative assistant for the Hotel and Restaurant Employees Union Local 69 in Long Island, New York. They also claimed that Pries has associated with Sonny Franzese, an influential member in the Colombo crime family in New York.

On February 6, 1981, Commito and Allu were again seen meeting with Frank D'Alfonso and Harry Riccobene in Philadelphia. During this meeting, Commito and Riccobene left the house and walked around the block three times while they spoke. They then re-entered the house.

When Commito departed, he was overheard mentioning Harrah's Hotel Casino in Atlantic City, New Jersey. He also said that ". . . arrangements have been made for an eight o'clock meeting at Bookbinder's; the accountant, Alan Cohen, will be there."

The Bookbinder's meeting took place just five days later on February 11. Present were Commito, Allu, D'Alfonso, local entertainer Jerry Blavat, and Alan Cohen, a Philadelphia accountant.

The Crime Commission was later able to obtain information on the purpose of the meeting from Alan Cohen in a private hearing. Cohen said that Commito discussed the financing of an Atlantic City building which he was trying to purchase to be the site of a health clinic to be used by members of the Teamsters Local 331. During the meeting, Commito telephoned a Teamster's official, Dick Kavner, in St. Louis, Missouri and introduced him to Cohen. Arrangements were then made for Cohen and Kavner to meet at Harrahs regarding the project.

**Allu has had several convictions for perjury in relation to his testimony during investigations into corruption in the Teamsters Union in New York City.*

**It is hypothesized that the reason for Allu's role was that the union being solicited to was in Atlantic City and the New York and Philadelphia crime families share control of that area.

Raymond "Long John" Martorano, long-time associate of murdered mob boss Angelo Bruno, with James Cox, President of the Amalgamated Meatcutters' Union and Theodore Manuele, the vice president of Pickwell Markets. *See page 20 for more details.*

Harry "Hunchback" Riccobene, a La Cosa Nostra family member, and Angelo Commito walking on a South Philadelphia street.

Angelo Commito and Frank D'Alfonso during one of Commito's visits to Philadelphia.

Cohen also detailed results from other meetings he had with Commito and his associates. He said that he first met Commito in April of 1980 when he was introduced to him by N. Steven Montrose. A meeting was held in Cohen's office between Montrose, John Allu and Commito.

According to Cohen, the discussion during this meeting involved the types of financing that Cohen could provide for clients. At the time, Cohen was not given the specifics of the project for which financing was needed.

During the summer of 1980, a second meeting was held at Palumbo's Nostalgia Room Restaurant in South Philadelphia. The participants at this meeting included Montrose, Cohen, Allu, Commito and D'Alfonso. As in the first meeting, only generalities were discussed.

In January of 1981, Cohen was contacted and a meeting was arranged at the coffee shop of the Bellevue Strafford Hotel in Philadelphia. Cohen met with Commito, Montrose and Allu. For the first time, Commito related the specifics of his plan.

Commito was attempting to market a prepaid health plan with the Teamsters Local 331 in Atlantic City. He wanted to purchase a building to house the medical facilities which would serve the union members. Cohen was asked to forward a letter to the attorney for the union outlining what services Cohen could provide, as the financing of the building was to be assured by the union health and welfare fund.

Teamsters Local 331 was a unit of the Chauffeurs, Warehousemen and Helpers of America and represented various employees of Harrah's Hotel Casino in Atlantic City.

About one week after the Bookbinder's meeting, Cohen met Teamsters officials Dick Kavner and Jack Miller at Harrah's. During this meeting, Kavner and Miller outlined the health plan they were attempting to put together for the approximately 2,000 members of the local union. The union needed between $4 and $7 million in loans for the project. Cohen, after reviewing the union's cash flow and repayment ability, decided to attempt to find financing for the project.

Cohen, however, was unable to get the financing, despite his approaches to several lenders. Consequently, Commito's plan fell through.

Frank D'Alfonso

Frank D'Alfonso is a major gambling figure and a significant associate of the Bruno/Testa/? crime family in Philadelphia.

D'Alfonso, of 821 South 9th Street, Philadelphia, has risen to power since the death of former Cosa Nostra boss Angelo Bruno in 1980. D'Alfonso is now active as the liaison for the Philadelphia Cosa Nostra with other organized crime families.

Michelene D'Alfonso, Frank's wife, owned the South Philadelphia restaurant, Cous', at which Bruno had his last meal before being murdered. Harry "Hunchback" Riccobene, a member of the Cosa Nostra family, has operated a sizeable loan-shark business out of a storefront owned by D'Alfonso.

D'Alfonso has run bingo games for St. Paul's Roman Catholic Church in South Philadelphia. In November of 1980, the Philadelphia Police raided one of those games and confiscated 24 illegal slot machines. No arrests were made.

On October 29, 1981, D'Alfonso was brutally attacked on the street near Cous' Restaurant. He was reportedly beaten with a baseball bat and a tire iron, and suffered several major injuries. It is not known if this had any connection to his role in La Cosa Nostra.

** Frank D'Alfonso and Harry Riccobene were subpoenaed to testify before the Pennsylvania Crime Commission but they refused to testify on the basis of their Constitutional privileges.*

Helping the Union

In the course of their marketing effort, Commito and Allu were also present at a meeting with union officials and Harrah's management which resolved some employee complaints.

John Allan, the manager of Harrah's, told law enforcement officials that during the winter of 1980, commissary workers at Harrah's had various complaints. The employees were members of Local 331 and the hotel's management entered into negotiations to resolve the complaints with Local 331 representatives Jack Miller and Bob Cericola.

The problem could not be resolved and, in an effort to settle the dispute, Allan met with Francis Kelly, the director of Harrah's Casino Relations department; Harold J. Gibbons, International Teamsters vice president; Angelo Commito; John Allu; and Richard Costello, a labor consultant from New York.

The meeting had been arranged after Kelly, attending a function in New York in January of 1981, met a former friend, Richard Costello, and Commito. Kelly told the men of the union problem. Costello and Commito said they could be of assistance in the negotiations and the meeting was arranged.

At another meeting the same day, the health plan project was discussed, but no decision was made at that time. Both Gibbons, the International vice president, and Commito spoke in favor of the health plan. John Allan later said that Commito was like a "godson to Gibbons."

It is interesting to note that during the time negotiations were in progress, Allan was introduced to Frank D'Apolito. D'Apolito was at Harrah's in the company of Allu and Richard Costello. According to New Jersey officials, D'Apolito is a member of the Gambino crime family in New York. D'Apolito is affiliated with the Teamsters Local 854 in New York. Among his close associates are Anthony Zappi, a Gambino crime family member and secretary of Local 854 and Ettore Zappi, a capo in the Gambino family.

In addition, it should be noted that Angelo Commito was introduced by Steven Montrose to Wendell Young, president of Local 1357 of the United Food and Commercial Workers Union in Philadelphia. Commito attempted to market a foot care program for Local 1357 members, but Young was not interested in this program.

ORGANIZED CRIME ASSOCIATION WITH UNION HEALTH PLANS

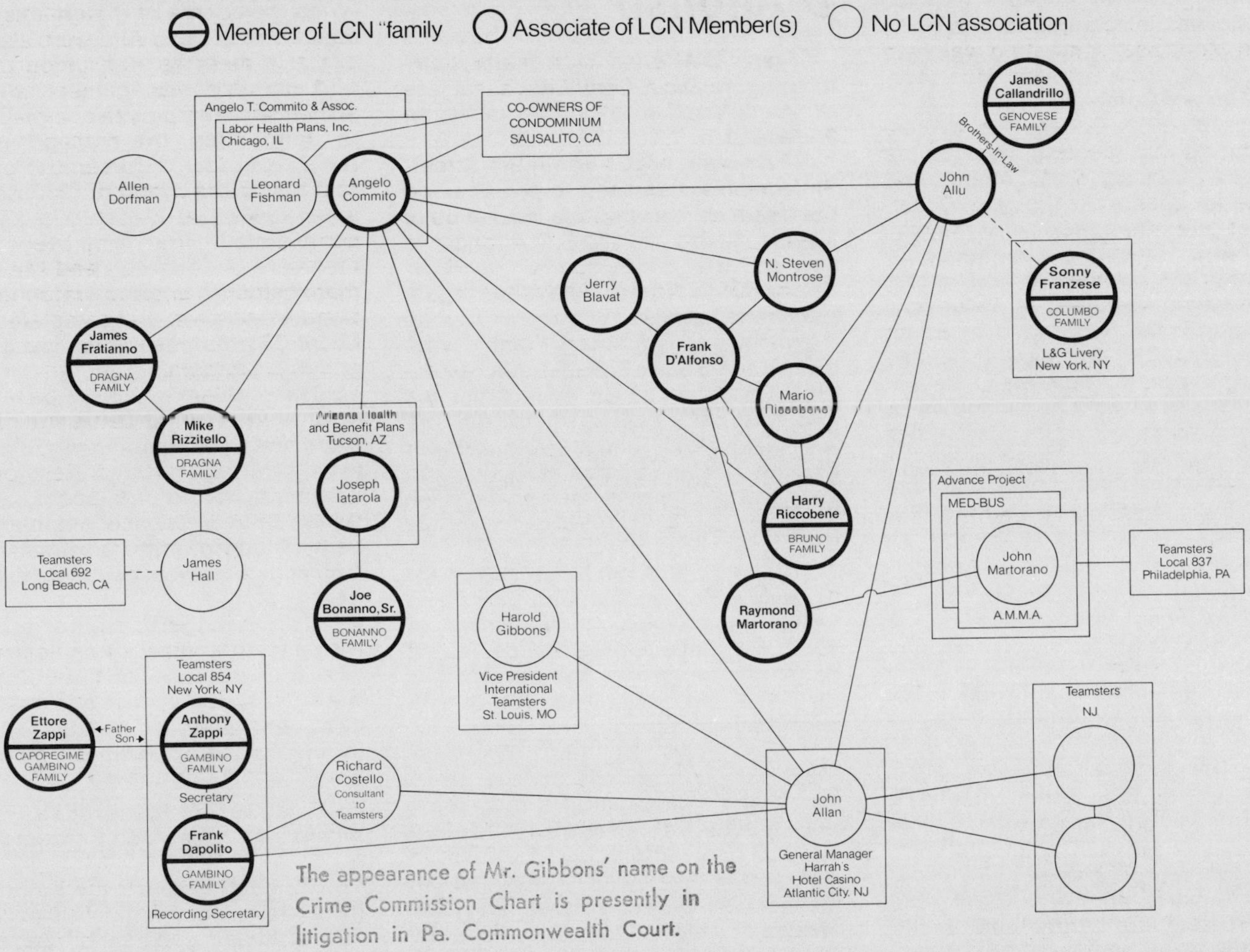

Coast to Coast Connections

Because of Commito's interest in obtaining health contracts in this area, the Crime Commission investigated some of his out-of-state dealings.

Labor Health Plans, Commito's company, is located at 230 North Michigan Avenue in Chicago, Illinois. It was incorporated on March 30, 1973.

The president of the company at the time of its incorporation was Leonard Fishman. Angelo Commito was its secretary and Anthony Ponzio was treasurer. Commito and Nancy Fishman were also listed as directors.

Also in 1973, Commito formed another company known as Angelo T. Commito and Associates. Official records indicate that Commito, Anthony Ponzio and Leonard Fishman were the principals in the venture. This business was an insurance agency.

Leonard Fishman, Commito's partner, is a close business associate of Alan Dorfman, a key advisor for the International Brotherhood of Teamsters' Central States' Pension Fund. In 1972, Dorfman was convicted of conspiring to accept a $55,000 kickback in return for arranging a $1.5 million loan from the Pension Fund. Dorfman was sentenced to one year in prison.

Commito and Fishman were also involved in another corporation called the Arizona Health and Benefit Plans, Inc. This corporation was formed on August 4, 1975 by Lawrence P. D'Antonio, Esq. and Garven W. Videen.

Fishman was listed as president of this corporation and Commito was listed as vice-president. Law enforcement authorities in California and Arizona have indicated that one of the directors of this corporation was Joseph Iatarola, a bodyguard and associate of organized crime figure Joseph Bonanno. Iatarola's name, however, was removed from the corporation shortly after an interview with the Federal Bureau of Investigation. Iatarola acknowledged to law enforcement officials during a 1975 interview that he had been involved in the corporation but that he had disassociated himself from Commito.

Arizona Health and Benefit Plans Inc. had obtained prepaid dental contracts with labor groups representing Tucson City employees. Investigation by Arizona authorities revealed that the funds for the city employees were being directed into a trust account in a Phoenix, Arizona bank and then to Labor Health Plans in Chicago.

Investigative background material regarding Angelo Commito also revealed an association with Michael Rizzitello, a key member of the Dragna crime family in Southern California.

Law enforcement authorities in California have revealed that in November 1977, Commito and Rizzitello met with a California dentist; Gunder Hansen, who was a union organizer for Teamsters Local 692; and James Hall, former business agent for Local 692. The meeting took place at a restaurant in San Pedro, California. Prior to this meeting, Commito had met with Rizzitello and William Darnold in August of

1977 at a Los Angeles delicatessen. Darnold has been identified by California officials as an explosives expert.

In addition, Commito met with Aladena "Jimmy the Weasel" Fratianno, former co-boss of the Dragna Family in September of 1977.

At the Crime Commission's public hearings on July 28, 1981, Fratianno testified about his introduction to Commito through Mike Rizzitello. Fratianno had become a government witness in 1977 after he learned that there was a murder contract out for him. Following are some of Fratianno's statements about Commito during the Commission's hearing.*

Q: Mr. Fratianno, do you know an individual by the name of Angelo Commito?

A: Yes, sir.

Q: And how did you know Mr. Commito?

A: Well, Mike Rizzitello introduced me to Commito, and I don't know if it was late '66 or early '77 (sic). I don't actually recall the time.

Q: And who was Mike Rizzitello?

A: . . . He was a capo in our family. (N. T. 121)

Q: What was the purpose of Mr. Commito's introduction to you by Mr. Rizzitello?

A: Well, Mike wanted, asked me about getting him to meet some union people so he can put out these programs that he had. He had some different kind of medical programs.

Q: By "medical programs," sir, are you referring to dental and health plans for union members, where contracts are made with the union itself for the services of the program to the benefit of the members of the union?

A: Yes. Well, not particularly dental or—they had eight or ten different programs; life insurance. And they had all kinds of programs.

Q: Mostly related to health and welfare benefits?

A: Right . . . .

Q: . . . What, if anything were you and Mr. Rizzitello to get out of the assistance you were giving to Mr. Commito, if he landed some of these plans?

A: Well, at that time Commito was giving Mike some money. . . . Commito did tell me that we would make a lot of money if we got any of these programs to the union. Now how much, I don't know . . . .

Fratianno then told of the introductions he made for Commito to various union officials.

***More of Fratianno's testimony can be found in Appendix B.*

Q: Now what, if anything, did you and Mr. Rizzitello do for Mr. Commito?

A: Well, I took him to one of the leaders of the Teamsters in San Francisco. I also took him to a fellow by the name of Rudy Tham. And I took him to a guy by the name of Tim Richards.

Q: . . . Who was Mr. Tham?

A: Well, Tham was the head of a local there. And he also was vice-president of the joint council.

Q: Do you know what particular locals he was the head of at the time that you brought Mr. Commito to him?

A: I think it was Local 856 . . .

Q: Was Mr. Tham to make any money out of this himself, if he was to give the work—the contract to Mr. Commito?

A: Yes, sir.

Q: And how did you know that?

A: Well, I told him he'd get some money from me.

Q: Who is Tim Richards?

A: Well, he had Local 80 or 85, I forget which one of the two it is. He also has a big local.

Q: Was it the same procedure: You were to introduce Mr. Commito to Mr. Richards, and if Mr. Commito got the contract, you and Mr. Rizzitello would receive money and some of it would be passed on to Mr. Richards?

A: That's correct.

Commito had obtained dental contracts with at least two other additional unions in the midwest. Labor Health Plans received a contract with the Teamsters Local 413 in Columbus, Ohio in 1975. This contract was negotiated by Commito and Vito Mango, then president of Local 413.

According to Mango, Commito "wined and dined" him prior to the signing of the contract. Commito also provided Mango with a trip to the Bahamas.

Mango later introduced Commito to John E. Scales, Business manager of Teamsters Local 423 in Columbus, Ohio. Commito was subsequently awarded a contract with this union in November of 1977. This contract was also for prepaid dental services.

High Teamsters Tie

During his testimony, Fratianno claimed that Jack Licavoli (aka Jack White), boss of the Cleveland La Cosa Nostra family, has a close association with Jack Presser, Vice-President of the International Brotherhood of Teamsters.

Q: Do you know whether Mr. Presser has any connection with Mr. Licavoli?

A: Yes, I do, sir.

Q: And what is that connection?

A: Well, at the time I was out, he never made a move unless, unless Jack White gave the okay. They practically run him.

Q: Jack White ran Presser?

A: The Cleveland family, whoever the boss is. It doesn't matter.

Q: Why, to your knowledge, would the Cleveland family have control over the vice-president, International Vice-president of the Teamsters, such as Mr. Presser?

A: Well, how do you think he got up there? That's how he got up there.

Fratianno attempted to use his influence with Presser to assist Commito in obtaining contracts with unions:

Q: Did you have a conversation with Mr. Presser concerning Angelo Commito?

A: Yes, sir.

Q: Would you please relate the circumstances of the conversation you had with Mr. Presser concerning Angelo Commito?

A: Well, I had some other business with Jackie Presser. In the same conversation I told him that Commito was—we were doing business with Commito, and that if he could help him in any way, it would mean money for us.

Q: What was Mr. Presser's response?

A: He said he would (do) what he can for him.

Although Fratianno was not aware if Commito obtained any contracts to supply health and welfare benefits to unions, his testimony did establish the close connection that Commito had with various organized crime figures. Fratianno, in fact, identified Commito as an organized crime associate.*

**It is interesting to note that in an address book found on the body of Carl Rizzo, an associate of the Magaddino Crime Family in Buffalo, N. Y., the name Angelo Commito, 619 West Randolph Street, Labor Health Plans of America was written. Rizzo was found garroted in the trunk of a car in April of 1980. A rope was looped around Rizzo's neck and then tied to his ankles so that as his body relaxed he strangled himself to death. A note apparently from Commito to Rizzo also found on the body read as follows: "This is a good friend with an interesting idea. An issue you can help her with. Please do take care, Angelo." Fratianno identified Rizzo as an LCN member.*

Chapter Three
A.M.M.A. Health Center Ties to Organized Crime

A.M.M.A. Health Center, Inc. Ties To Organized Crime

The involvement of local traditional organized crime figures in the delivery of health care services is demonstrated by the A.M.M.A. Health Center, Inc. A.M.M.A., a subsidiary of Advance Project Corporation, is located at 2001 South 29th Street in Philadelphia.*

A.M.M.A. is a Pennsylvania corporation which administers, on a prepaid basis, out-patient health care benefits for union members and employee groups. The corporation enlists the services of area physicians and clinics to perform out-patient treatment for union or employee groups. The union fund pays A.M.M.A. which, in turn, pays the physicians on a pre-arranged basis.

A.M.M.A. Health Center, Inc. was incorporated as the Golden Block Medical Center, Inc. at 3922-26 North 5th Street, Philadelphia. It was formed to act as a medical health clinic, mainly through the efforts of Joseph Martorano, a cousin to Raymond Martorano. Joseph Martorano was a licensed pharmacist in Pennsylvania. However, efforts to secure funding for this clinic were unsuccessful.

On October 26, 1978, a Certificate of Amendment was filed in the Pennsylvania Bureau of Corporations changing the name of Golden Block to the A.M.M.A. Health Center, Inc. The address of A.M.M.A. at that time was 739 South Broad Street, Philadelphia. The corporate papers listed Dr. Raymond Silk as president. The company's books and records, however, show John Martorano as president and Joseph Martorano as secretary.

**This location also houses John's Wholesale Distributors, Inc. and another Advance Project subsidiary, Med-Bus, Inc. John's Wholesale Distributors is a wholesale outlet for cigarettes and other tobacco products. Angelo Bruno, the assassinated former head of the Philadelphia Cosa Nostra, was employed by John's as a salesman. Other Bruno/Testa/? family members including Harry Riccobene and the murdered John Simore were also employed there. Med-Bus Inc. is a corporation that provides medical transportation service for aged and incapacitated individuals. Many Med-Bus clients are recipients of public assistance or some other form of government medical assistance. For more on Med-Bus, see page 25-6.*

John's Wholesale Distributors, Inc., at 2001 South 29th Street, is also the location of the A.M.M.A. Health Center, Inc.

In addition, John Martorano was a 55 percent owner of A.M.M.A. The location of A.M.M.A. at that time was also the location of the Broad Street Hospital, of which Silk was a principal and the medical director. According to Silk, he invested $2,500 in A.M.M.A. Joseph Martorano invested $2,000 and John Martorano invested $5,000. The location of A.M.M.A. was later moved to the 2001 South 29th Street location.

Dr. Silk also functioned as the medical director of A.M.M.A. His clinic, the Broad Street Hospital, was the largest of the clinics through which A.M.M.A. delivered health care.

The day-to-day activities of A.M.M.A. were originally operated by Joseph Martorano. He was, however, replaced by John Martorano in approximately February of 1979.

In addition to the above-mentioned individuals, the Crime Commission learned that Raymond Martorano was also involved in certain aspects of the A.M.M.A. business. Raymond "Long John" Martorano was a long-time associate of deceased mob boss Angelo Bruno and is recognized by many law enforcement authorities as an organized crime figure.

While Raymond Martorano's name does not appear as an owner or officer of A.M.M.A., evidence strongly suggests that he did have a role in the company.

James Cox, President of the United Food and Commercial Workers Union Local 196 (formerly the Amalgamated Meat Cutters), testified that Raymond Martorano had given him and Theodore Manuele, vice-president of Pickwell Markets, a tour of A.M.M.A. facilities in the hopes of procuring a contract for A.M.M.A.*

**The contract did not go through.*

Manuele denied, when interviewed by Commission agents, that he had been shown the facilities by Martorano, but later, in the Commission's public hearings, admitted it.

Furthermore, the Crime Commission obtained sworn testimony from a former employee of A.M.M.A. which clearly indicated Raymond Martorano's involvement in soliciting business for A.M.M.A. and in the operation of A.M.M.A. This former employee claimed to have been informed by one of the corporation's officers that Raymond Martorano was soliciting union business for A.M.M.A. and was the company's contact with various unions.

The former employee also stated that Martorano attended management meetings of A.M.M.A., has shown the office facilities to the representative of a union fund, and had questioned the employee about how many patients were being served at the various satellite clinics.

A final bit of evidence was obtained when the Pennsylvania Crime Commission subpoenaed the records of the A.M.M.A. Health Center and the company's cancelled checks were reviewed. Two checks were found which were, apparently, written as entertainment expenses for A.M.M.A. Check #146, written on November 14, 1978, to the D'Medici Restaurant in the amount of $235.35, had the names of several individuals in the margin, including that of Raymond Martorano. The corresponding check stub from the checkbook also contains the name of Raymond Martorano.

Check #137, written to Joseph Martorano in the amount of $32.00 dated November 10, 1978, also has several names listed on the margin of the check. Among these is the name "Raymond." The corresponding check stub contains several names, including that of Raymond Martorano.

Dr. Silk

Dr. Raymond Silk is a Philadelphia physician. He was temporarily suspended from participating in the public Medicare program in 1980 by the Pennsylvania Department of Welfare. Silk's suspension resulted from an investigation which alleged that he performed unnecessary surgical procedures and charged fees that were higher than they should have been. A subsequent agreement with the Department revoked the suspension and allowed Silk to participate subject to certain limitations. Silk resigned from A.M.M.A. in February, 1980.

In 1979, Dr. Silk, John Martorano and Dr. Paul Felix, a Philadelphia dentist, attempted to establish another outpatient and dental benefit company known as Life Check. Life Check was to be located in Atlantic City, New Jersey, and according to Silk, attempts were made to negotiate with the building trades council and security guard unions in that city. The program was never established according to Silk.

Medical Fraud

On July 1, 1981, Joseph Martorano, Jesse Gutman of Rydal, and Martin I. Askin of Philadelphia were sentenced for a forgery and conspriacy conviction. The three had operated the 817 Medical Clinic on North 42nd Street from May of 1975 to January of 1977. Although none were licensed physicians, they treated patients and then fraudulently billed State medical programs for more than $21,000. Gutman was sentenced to 11½ to 23 months in prison, 5 years probation, and a $3,500 fine; Martorano to 9 to 23 months in prison, 5 years probation, and a $2,500 fine; and Askin to 4 to 23 months in prison, 3 years probation, and a $1,000 fine.

In addition, Martorano was indicted on June 9, 1981, by a federal grand jury on charges of making false Medicare and medical claims in the sale of electronic nerve stimulators to elderly persons. Martorano operated a firm known as TNS Medical Dynamics out of his residence. Claims totalling $7,000 were submitted in 1978 to the U. S. Department of Health and Human Services.

The Only Contract

The only contract that A.M.M.A. Health Center, Inc. has secured since its inception was with the Health and Welfare Fund of Local 837 of the Industrial Workers Union, an affiliate of the International Brotherhood of Teamsters. The offices of this fund are located at 8033 Old York Road, Philadelphia, PA.

The Health and Welfare Fund constitutes the contributions of employers (pursuant to collective bargaining agreement) that are to be used to purchase various health, medical, insurance and welfare benefits for the approximately 2,000 union members and their dependents.

The Health and Welfare Fund is governed by a board of six trustees who make the ultimate decisions in the overall management of the fund.* The day-to-day operations of the Health and Welfare Fund are governed by fund administrator Howard H. Bucher. Bucher has held the position of administrator since 1966.

The A.M.M.A. program was introduced to the trustees by Howard Bucher and Pasquale Tavella, who was then the President of Local 837. Bucher testified before the Pennsylvania Crime Commission that prior to the acceptance of the A.M.M.A. program, he contacted other health care providers such as Blue Cross/Blue Shield, and he found the costs of such programs to be prohibitive. Bucher did not, however, obtain written bids from these companies, and made the contacts by telephone.

Bucher further stated that when A.M.M.A. was originally being considered he had been dealing with Joseph Martorano, but after Martorano's disassociation with A.M.M.A. all transactions were conducted through John Martorano.

The contract with A.M.M.A. was ultimately approved by the board of trustees. However, several of its members later admitted to the Crime Commission that they were not very familiar with the specifics of the A.M.M.A. contract, and one stated that the board acted as a rubber stamp operation for the proposals of Howard Bucher.

**Three of the trustees represent the union and three represent management.*

Under the terms of the contract, the Health and Welfare Fund would pay $8.50 each month for each union member. In return the union members and their dependents could utilize the outpatient and diagnostic services of the participating physicians and clinics. The contract was signed by Joseph Martorano on behalf of A.M.M.A. and by Pasquale Tavella for the fund.

In October of 1980, the contract with A.M.M.A. was renewed for a term of five years at the increased cost of $10 a month for each union member. The entire contract renewal consisted of a one-page letter dated May 8, 1980, requesting the above terms. According to Bucher, this contract was approved in October 1980. A copy of this contract was signed by John Martorano and Howard Bucher.

A.M.M.A. Wages

A review of records revealed that wages paid by A.M.M.A. for the period of October 1 to December 31, 1978 for the five employees of the company was reported as $54,518.76. Key employee wages for the three months were as follows:

John Martorano	**$22,675**
Raymond Silk	**12,025**
Joseph Martorano	**18,600**

A.M.M.A. had no other contracts with unions or employee groups in that period. The profit for 1978 shown in the utilization report combined with the cost of administration equals $49,448.50. There appears to be, therefore, a discrepancy of over $5,000 between what monies A.M.M.A. spent on employees and what funds it had to spend. Moreover, other records for 1978 show John Martorano receiving a salary $2,000 over what was carried on the first records.

Calendar 1980 records show $45,848.33 in wages paid to up to four employees. $30,910 of this was paid to John Martorano. The utilization report for this period shows $32,500 as the cost of administration, which is approximately $13,000 less than A.M.M.A. actually spent.

Utilization Reports

Declining Profits

The profits which A.M.M.A. claimed to have obtained through its management of health care services for Local 837 can be seen by reviewing its utilization reports.

The utilization reports generally described for the fund members the number of office visits as well as the value of these visits and the value of laboratory and X-ray services. The reports also indicated the costs of administration and further indicated the net profit for A.M.M.A. in relation to the contract. A copy of the submitted utilization report which covers the years 1978 and 1979 is found on page 23.*

The report shows 387 office visits from October 1978 to December 1978. The reported value of the office visits was $14,679. The reported value of laboratory and X-ray services was $2,098 for a total value of $16,777. A.M.M.A. showed the cost of administration as $9,285.57.

The fund had paid premiums of $66,325.50 for the period covered and A.M.M.A. reported a profit of $40,262.93. A.M.M.A. did not detail the elements of cost of administration and, as can be observed in the report, A.M.M.A. also did not give a thorough breakdown of the services rendered.

The report for the following year, 1979, indicated a total of 3,234 office visits for a total value of $122,745. Laboratory and X-ray services for that period were valued at $39,726 for a total value of $162,471. A.M.M.A. claimed $32,847.29 as the cost of administration. (See page 23.)

The premiums paid by the fund for this period was $234,623.50 and A.M.M.A. reported a net profit of $39,305.21.

The utilization report covering the year of 1980 can be observed on page 00. The report indicated that office visits numbered 4,164 for a total value of $122,047. The value of X-ray and laboratory services was portrayed as $16,343 for a total value of $198,390. A.M.M.A.'s cost of administration was $32,500 and when subtracted from the fund premium payment of $235,707, A.M.M.A. was supposedly left with an annual net profit of $4,817.

The report from these three years show a dramatic decrease in profits, both in dollars and as a percentage of the whole. The following chart summarizes the percentages of costs (office visits and lab fees), administration fees and net profits.

A.M.M.A. Contract With Local 837
A.M.M.A. Claims of utilization of monies
in their relationship to total premiums paid

	Value of Services (Doctors & Labs)	Administrative Fees	Profits
1978	25%	13%	62%
1979	69%	13%	18%
1980	84%	15%	1%

A.M.M.A. Costs
Reported vs. Actual

	1978	1979	1980
Reported Value of Services	**$16,777**	**$162,471**	**$198,390**
Actual Billings	**4,633**	**29,994**	**88,296**
Reported Administration	**9,285**	**32,847**	**32,500**
Prepayment from Union	**66,325.50**	**234,623.50**	**235,707**
Reported Profit	**40,263**	**39,305**	**4,817**
Monies Remaining*	**$52,406**	**$171,782**	**$114,911**

**Derived from adding actual billings with reported administrative costs and subtracting that sum from the premiums paid by the union.*

It should also be reiterated that the original contract between A.M.M.A. and Local 837 ran for two years and was renegotiated in 1980.

Local 837 officials apparently wondered how A.M.M.A. was managing to stay in business with such low profits in 1980. Howard Bucher testified that, at a June 1981 meeting, A.M.M.A. told his trustees that the value of doctors and laboratory fees listed was not money actually paid by A.M.M.A. A.M.M.A. did not, however, explain why then those figures were used in their reports to determine annual net profits and no one asked.

Falsified Reports

The Crime Commission has determined that the figures reported to the Health and Welfare Fund of Local 837 by A.M.M.A. were significantly higher than the actual figures.

To make this determination, the Commission used several sets of documents. The primary source of the figures was from the doctors' or clinics' records themselves. A secondary source of information was from ledgers maintained by A.M.M.A. which were obtained under subpoena. The third source of information was from copies of billings from various doctors and clinics maintained by A.M.M.A. which were obtained by the Crime Commission under subpoena. The fourth source of information, which was used only in a few relatively minor instances, were the checking account records of A.M.M.A. obtained by subpoena of the Pennsylvania Crime Commission.

The actual reported figures are shown on page 23 and 24. These figures relate to both the number of office visits and the value of services rendered.

For 1978, the Commission was able to document 308 office visits with a total value of $4,633. This contrasts sharply to the utilization report figures of 387 visits and value of services of $16,777. The documented visits represent only 79 percent of those reported. Documented billings were only 27 percent of the claimed value of services reported to the union.

For 1979, the Commission was able to document 1,677 visits and $29,994 in billings. These figures are even more disparate from reported figures than those in 1978. Documented visits represent 51 percent of the figures reported. Documented billings were only 18 percent of the claimed value of services reported to the union.

For 1980, 3,522 office visits were documented, which is 84 percent of the 4,164 number of visits reported. $88,296 in documented billings were found, which represents 44 percent of

**It is interesting to note that the reports of utilized services for 1978, 1979 and 1980 were not submitted to the union until 1981.*

A.M.M.A. HEALTH CENTER, INC. P. O. Box 20135 Philadelphia, Pa. 19145 (215) 389-0350

April 9, 1981

Board of Trustees
Teamsters Industrial Union
Local 837, Health & Welfare Fund

ATTN: Howard Bucher, Administrator

RE: Utilization Report for Medical Out-Patient Services

Dear Mr. Bucher:

The following is a summary of claims activity for participants of Local 837 for the period of October, 1978 through December, 1978 and January, 1979 through December, 1979.

Average number of claims per month	270
Average dollar of value per claim	$50.15
Total premium paid, January 1979 through December 1979	$234,623.50
Total dollar value of services rendered same period	162,471.00
	72,152.50
Cost of Administration (14%)	32,847.29
Annual Net Profit	$ 39,305.21

I hope that this summary will be satisfactory to your needs.

Thank you for your cooperation in this matter.

Sincerely,

JOHN MARTORANO
ADMINISTRATOR

A.M.M.A. HEALTH CENTER, INC. P. O. Box 20135 Philadelphia, Pa. 19145 (215) 389-0350

February 17, 1981

Board of Trustees
Teamsters Industrial Union
Local 837, Health and Welfare Fund

ATTN: Mr. Howard Bucher, Administrator

RE: Utilization Report for Medical Out-Patient Services

Dear Mr. Bucher:

The following is a summary of claims activity for participants of Local 837 for the period of January 1980 through December 1980. This report shows the total number of claims per month, the relative dollar value of office visits per month, the dollar value of laboratory and radiological services rendered per month, and finally the total dollar value of all services rendered to your members. The report also shows the average number of claims per month, and the average dollar value per claim. Injectibles administered to patients during office visits are included with the total dollar value of laboratory and radiology.

Average number of claims per month	347
Average dollar value per claim	$ 47.65
Total premium paid, January 1980 through December 1980	$ 235,707.00
Total dollar value of services rendered same period	198,390.00
	$ 37,317.00
Cost of Administration (14%)	32,500.00
Annual Net Profit	$ 4,817.00

I hope that this summary will be satisfactory for your needs.

Thank you for your cooperation in this matter.

Sincerely,

John Martorano
Administrator

the $198,390 in value of services reported to the union.

The utilization reports from this 28-month period show a total of 5,307 visits and $377,638 in services billed. The Commission was only able to document 2,478 visits and $122,923 as the value of services performed.

The Union's Acceptance

According to testimony by various local 837 Health and Welfare Fund trustees, they had to rely upon the reports provided by A.M.M.A. and never questioned their accuracy.

Howard Bucher, the Fund's administrator, told the Commission that John Martorano had also told him use of the services was high. Bucher stated: "He (John Martorano) told me . . . that in the two years, in that time it was a year and a half since the contract was in its inception. The members of the Local 837 were utilizing the outpatient facilities more and more. And his costs, not only because of utilization, but his costs by the doctors to provide the services to our union members is going up."

Bucher also testified that such utilization reports would affect the negotiations for new contracts, such as the renegotiation of the A.M.M.A. contract in 1980.

> "If in fact I thought that the program in 1980 was not being utilized and was not a viable benefit we were providing to our members, then I wouldn't have considered extending the contract or entering into it again, because it would not have been a used function or benefit."

Based on utilization reports given to Bucher and the trustees of the fund, Bucher wrote to the trustees that the fund's participation in the A.M.M.A. program was justified based on the figures indicated in the reports. Referring specifically to the report that covered the calendar year for 1980, Bucher made the following statement in his letter:

> "I am enclosing herewith a cost breakdown and benefits payment program under our agreement with the A.M.M.A. Health Center, Inc. Please note that out of the total premium paid by our Fund of $235,000.00, our membership's utilization amounted to almost $200,000.00. From an administrative point of view, it is my judgment that this high benefit utilization more than justifies our participation in this program. The enclosed information has been provided by A.M.M.A. pursuant to a request made by this office."*

As is clear from the foregoing, A.M.M.A. substantially altered the actual figures of services and put inflated figures in the utilization reports. It appears to have been done without the knowledge of the officials of the Health and Welfare Fund.

A $16,000 Mystery

A review of the books and records of A.M.M.A. revealed what appeared to be an attempt by A.M.M.A. to secure a contract with Local 36 of the Service Employees International Union Health and Welfare Fund (SEIU). This union represents window cleaners and maintenance workers and is located in the Robinson Building in Philadelphia.

According to documents of the union, the administrator of this union's benefit plans and Health and Welfare Fund was Timothy P. Smith.* Smith operated an entity known as TPS Enterprises, Suite 1214, 42 South 15th Street in Philadelphia. This is also the location of the SEIU Health and Welfare Fund office.

While no contract with the SEIU fund could be found in the A.M.M.A. records and no members of this union have been treated by the A.M.M.A. participating physicians, the Commission found a letter in the A.M.M.A. books and records regarding this matter. In this letter (see page 00) dated August 14, 1978 to Joseph Martorano, it is stated that a $4,000 deposit was enclosed as part of the outpatient premiums due A.M.M.A. from SEIU. The letter is signed Timothy P. Smith.

A review of the A.M.M.A. cash receipt's journals indicates that this check was deposited on August 18, 1978 in the A.M.M.A. account. The journal also shows the notation T.S.P. Enterprises rather than T.P.S. Enterprises. In addition, two other checks were entered on the A.M.M.A. journals as having been received from T.S.P. These checks were as follows: September 20, 1978 in the amount of $4,000, and November 6, 1978 in the amount of $8,000. The total amount is $16,000.

This money was the first income of the A.M.M.A. Health Center, Inc.

Agents of the Pennsylvania Crime Commission interviewed representatives of the SEIU Health and Welfare Fund and have determined that the union did not have a contract with A.M.M.A. and had never, in fact, ever heard of A.M.M.A. Agents of the Crime Commission also reviewed the disbursement journals of the fund for the above time frame and these journals did not reflect any payments to A.M.M.A. from the union.

James Cox, President of Local 196 of the Amalgamated Meatcutters Union (UF&CWU) testified that when he was speaking with Dr. Silk in 1979, he was led to believe that a window cleaner's union was associated with the A.M.M.A. program.

The reason for these payments by Smith have not been ascertained. Timothy Smith was dismissed as the fund administrator in the spring of 1979 and T.P.S. Enterprises went out of business shortly thereafter.

**Timothy P. Smith was convicted on 8 counts of embezzlement and two counts of failure to file tax returns in September of 1981. He received four months in a halfway house, five years probation and was ordered to make restitution of $86,000.*

Ledger-de-Main

A.M.M.A. apparently enjoyed a close financial relationship with companies owned or controlled by the Martoranos.

As was mentioned before, A.M.M.A. was a subsidiary of Advance Project Corporation. Another Advance subsidiary was Med-Bus, which shares the same address (2001 So. 29th Street) with A.M.M.A.

Med-Bus, Inc. was originally founded by Joseph Martorano, Sam Wilson of Ardmore and Joseph Alston of Philadelphia. (See page 29 for Alston's connection to another health care provider). The original corporate address was 1616 Walnut Street, but it later moved to South 29th Street building, which houses John's Wholesale Distributors, Inc. Dr. Raymond Silk was also an investor in Med-Bus.

Records of A.M.M.A. subpoenaed by the Crime Commission showed $128,014.16 in interest-free loans made by A.M.M.A. to Med-Bus between 1978 and 1980. These loans, according to the company's accountant, were not secured and have not been repaid.

Interestingly, profits reported by A.M.M.A. to the union (see Utilization Reports) for 1978, 1979 and 1980 amount to only $84,385.14, yet it was able to loan over $128,000 to its sister company.

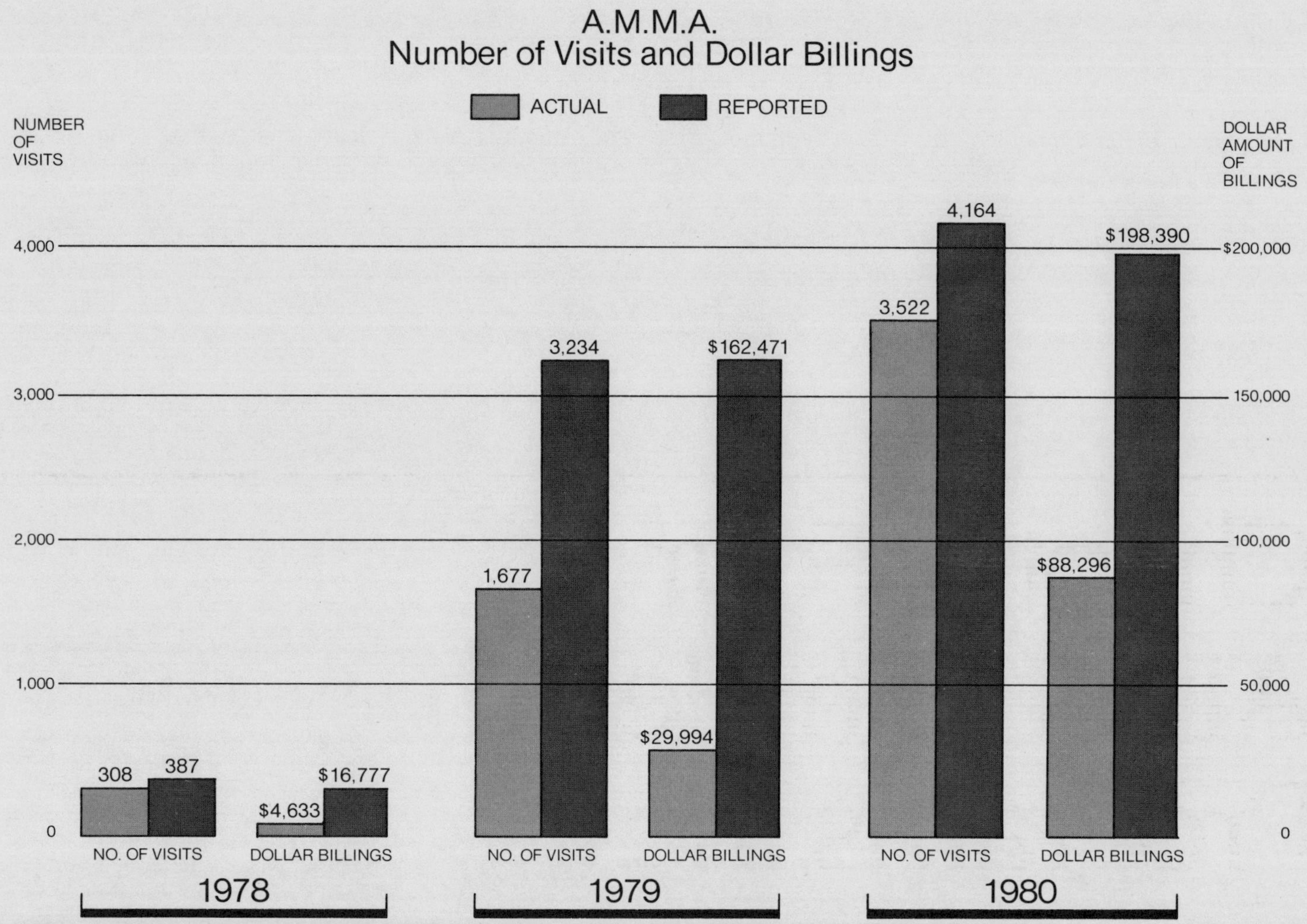

In addition, the records showed that A.M.M.A. paid a $90,000 management fee to Med-Bus in 1979, although records show no money changing hands.

Since A.M.M.A.'s records show a net income of $87,300 that year and Med-Bus suffered a loss of $92,387, both companies showed a year-end loss after the transfer. As a result, A.M.M.A. successfully avoided paying state taxes on its profits.

A.M.M.A. also loaned John Martorano $25,000 on March 6, 1981. On that same date, Martorano loaned his other business, John's Wholesale Distributors, $32,000. On March 12, Martorano received a check for $25,000 from John's Wholesale and issued a check for the same amount to Evelyn Martorano, his brother Raymond's wife. As of September 1981, A.M.M.A. had not been repaid.

As noted previously, A.M.M.A. rented space at 2001 South 29th Street. This location is owned by John Martorano (majority owner of A.M.M.A.) and his wife, Theresa. From February to May of 1979, A.M.M.A. books indicate that it paid John Martorano $500 a month for the rent on apparently only one room.

In June of 1979, however, the rent escalated by 700 percent to $3,500 per month.

Another tenant of the building, Med-Bus, paid Martorano $500 per month for its space until June of 1979. The rent then escalated to $1,750 per month. According to the company's accountant, A.M.M.A. and Med-Bus share the same office.

John's Wholesale, the primary tenant of the building, paid only $1,000 per month in rent until mid-1980, at which time it began paying $2,000 per month.

Both John and Raymond Martorano were subpoenaed to appear before the Crime Commission but they declined to testify on the basis of their Constitutional privileges.

Chapter Four
American Health Programs, Inc.

American Health Programs, Inc.: A Success Story

The Pennsylvania Crime Commission's investigation of American Health Programs, Inc. (AHP) uncovered questionable marketing techniques, falsified utilization reports and suspicious loans and investments to companies and individuals with ties to AHP.

Although no direct links were found between AHP and traditional organized crime figures, evidence was obtained which shows that AHP provided inflated benefit utilization reports to unions in order to ensure the successful renewal of its contracts with these unions.

American Health Programs, Inc. was formed in 1975 as a Delaware corporation by Dr. Charles Kravitz and Claude Collier. AHP was originally located at 1950 Street Road in Cornwells Heights, Pennsylvania, but later was relocated to its present office at One Neshaminy Interplex, Suite 106, Trevose, Pennsylvania.

In 1977, Kravitz, a Philadelphia area dentist, wanted to obtain full ownership of AHP and therefore bought out Collier. In March 1977, when Collier needed money, Kravitz made Collier a cash offer of $90,000 for his shares of AHP and Collier accepted, leaving Kravitz as sole stockholder of AHP.

Kravitz did not have the $90,000 in cash at that time, and as a result Kravitz raised $40,000 through personal savings and bank loans. In addition, Carol Lozanoff, Kravitz' receptionist and secretary, loaned AHP $50,000.*

In return for Lozanoff's loan, Kravitz agreed to pay Lozanoff a salary equal to his own at AHP and make her an officer of AHP. Lozanoff had been earning approximately $130 per week in salary. Her new base salary, as that of Kravitz, was $70,000 annually plus bonuses.

American Health Programs, Inc., commonly referred to as AHP, is a company which creates and administers dental, vision and drug prescription plans on a contract basis for unions and employee groups. The most significant portion of its business pertains to dental programs. In order to operate its dental programs, AHP has a network of participating dentists who provide the dental services.

**Lozanoff obtained these funds from three bank loans totaling $35,200 and $14,800 in savings.*

AHP operates on a fixed-fee per family (capitation) basis as opposed to the more traditional fee-for-service basis. In its programs, AHP assigns patients who are being serviced under contracts to participating dentists who agree to treat these patients at a fixed fee per family per month. Once assigned, AHP pays the participating dentists their monthly fees each month regardless of whether or not they treat any patients.*

The theory behind this approach to dentistry is that it will motivate the participating dentists to bring their patients to a state of good dental health as quickly as possible after which the dentists can look forward to collecting their monthly fees while providing minimal services.

AHP has been the major non-insurance company prepaid dental benefit provider in southeastern Pennsylvania. At one point, it considered expanding into New Jersey, using a Margate condominium as a branch office.

In the past several years, AHP has had four major contracts. In April of 1976, it signed a contract for services with the Pennsylvania Social Services Union, Pennsylvania Employment Securities Employees Association (PSSU/PESEA) which represents about 12,000 Commonwealth of Pennsylvania employees. That contract was in force for approximately one year.

From August 15, 1976 to August 15, 1978, AHP had a dental contract with the Delaware Valley Health and Welfare Fund of the Retail Clerks Union. After August 1978, this contract was continued on a month-to-month basis through December 1980. The annual cost of this contract was approximately $250,000, and it serviced about 3,000 union members.

On March 23, 1977, AHP signed a three-year contract with District Council 33 of AFSCME, the American Federation of State, County, and Municipal Employees. In March 1980, the contract was renewed for an additional three years. The annual cost of this contract, which serviced about 17,000 union members, was $2.4 million a year.

**It should be noted that AHP does not remit any payment to the participating dentists until a patient contacts AHP requesting dental services. The union premium payments remain with AHP until such time.*

On October 15, 1978, AHP signed a one-year dental, vision, and drug prescription contract with Police Health Administration, Inc., a corporation established to administer dental, vision, and drug prescription benefits for the Philadelphia Fraternal Order of Police, Lodge #5. In October 1979, PHA renewed its contract with AHP for two years. The contracts, which service about 8,000 union members, costs approximately $4.2 million a year.

AHP also had a contract with the International Brotherhood of Teamsters Local 169 at Leaseway Warehouses, Incorporated in Cornwells Heights. That contract was awarded in the spring of 1976.

The following sections of this report document, in each of these contracts, the questionable business methods of American Health Programs, Inc.

Cast of Characters

Philadelphia dentist Dr. Charles Kravitz and Claude Collier incorporated American Health Plans, Inc. in 1975. Kravitz bought out Collier's shares in 1977.

Robert Fluehr, an insurance salesman who had been involved in HCA, NADP and DDS, is AHP's marketing representative. Fluehr is the brother-in-law of Wendell Young, who heads the Retail Clerks Union Local 1357, with which AHP obtained a contract. Prior to his involvement with AHP, Fluehr was affiliated with the Retail Clerks Union in Philadelphia.

Carol P. Lozanoff, who had been Dr. Kravitz's secretary, provided some funds to Kravitz to buy Collier out of AHP. As a result, she was given a salary and bonuses equal to Kravitz's. She was also responsible for colating the information on usage for the company's utilization reports to the unions.

Dr. Sanford Roth, who had been involved in Dental Delivery Services, also became employed by AHP as its Director of Professional Relations. Through Roth, Dr. Kravitz was introduced to Berle Schiller, Esq., who aided AHP in getting the Pennsylvania Social Services Union contract.

HCA: A Spawning Ground

Health Corporation of America (HCA) was formed as a Delaware corporation in 1972. It began when North American Dental Plans Inc., a Pennsylvania Corporation, was consolidated with a Delaware entity, Capital Resources Industries Inc. In October of 1972, NADP was reincorporated in Pennsylvania as a wholly owned subsidiary of its holding company, HCA, for the purpose of operating, administering and designing prepaid dental plans. HCA and NADP were established by Joseph R. Cusamano of Devon, Pennsylvania and were originally located in King of Prussia, but later relocated to the Valley Forge Executive Mall in Wayne.

The executive vice president and secretary for NADP was John David Garner.* As noted in Chapter 1 of this report, NADP had obtained a contract with Local 170 of the Hotel and Restaurant Workers Employees Union in Camden, New Jersey. An investigation by the New Jersey State Commission of Investigation revealed a close connection with organized crime figures in relation to that contract.

During the early stages of HCA's operation, Cusumano contracted with Gary Garramone to market the HCA/NADP program. Garramone* was then operating through National Corporate Consultants (NCC) and received approximately $50,000 for his services. According to Cusamano, Garramone did not bring any business into HCA. NCC was located in Upper Darby, PA.

In September of 1972, NADP obtained a dental contract with the Tri-State Health and Welfare Fund of the Retail Clerks Union. This union later became known as the United Food and Commercial Workers Union (UF & CWU). The Tri-State Fund represented about 14,000 workers.

At the time NADP received this contract, one of the company's employees was Robert Fluehr, the brother-in-law of Wendell Young, chairman of the Health and Welfare Fund's board of trustees. Fleuhr, of Philadelphia, was later involved in another health provider known as AHP. (For more on this connection, see page 00).

According to Louis Mattucci, D.D.S., of Philadelphia, he was contacted by Wendell Young to review the various dental plans that were being considered by the health and welfare fund. Dr. Mattucci placed these proposals in order of priority and his top recommendation was for the selection of the NADP program.

Subsequent to this review that Mattucci conducted for Young, he obtained a position with NADP. As part of his position, Mattucci made the formal NADP proposal to the health and welfare fund board of trustees.

In 1976, North American Dental Plans was fined $50,000 by the New Jersey Board of Dentistry in connection with a consent decree the firm signed to restructure its operation to correct what the board termed as defects in procedures, design offer, and the administration of its dental plans.

In 1974, several of the HCA and NADP employees left and established a company to compete with HCA and NADP. Among them were Dr. Louis Mattucci and Dr. Charles Kravitz. The newly formed corporation was known as Dental Delivery Systems (DDS). DDS, like NADP, administered prepaid dental services plans for union or employee groups. Robert Fleuhr also left HCA and became the director of marketing for DDS.

Dental Delivery Systems was incorporated in New Jersey in 1973. At that time, its principal place of business was 101 North Lakeview Drive, Gibbsboro, N. J.

In 1973, DDS filed an application in the State Bureau of Corporations to do business in Pennsylvania. Mattucci signed the application as president and Kravitz signed as secretary.*

While at DDS, Kravitz attempted to secure several large contracts including a contract with AFSCME District Council 33 in Philadelphia and the Pennsylvania Social Services Union.

It is interesting to note that minutes of a board of directors meeting for DDS dated October 3, 1974 listed Steven Sheller, Esq. and Berle Schiller, Esq. as marketing agents for DDS.* Schiller, a Philadelphia attorney, is the nephew of former Pennsylvania Governor Milton Shapp. Sheller was legal co-counsel for the Pennsylvania Social Services Union board of trustees.

Dental Delivery Systems attempted to obtain the contract with the Tri-State Fund of the Retail Clerks Union. This effort was led by Mattucci, who had reviewed the dental programs for Tri-State when it originally awarded the contract to NADP.

Mattucci, Dr. Bertram Serota, David Spratt and Claude Collier formed a company known as Health Systems Management Inc. (HSM). HSM was then to utilize DDS as its primary contractor for the dental program. Mattucci testified that HSM was formed at the suggestion of Wendell Young, President of Local 1357 of the Retail Clerks and a member of the Tri-State fund board. According to Mattucci, this was done to obtain the contract after it was taken away from NADP, but this never occurred.

As a result of internal problems, Mattucci resigned from DDS. Kravitz left to form his own corporation, American Health Programs.

**In July of 1974, Garramone was convicted, along with several other individuals, of federal gambling charges in connection with the operation of an interstate sports betting business. Also convicted were Robert J. Lumio, former secretary/treasurer of Local 54 of the Hotel, Restaurant and Bartenders Union in Atlantic City, NJ; Albert J. Catalano, Jr.; and Emilio Joseph Tramontino, Jr. Garramone also attempted to arrange gambling junkets to Las Vegas in 1976 through National Corporate Consultants.*

**In addition to Kravitz and Mattucci, other principals or investors in DDS were Dr. Peter Cassalia, Dr. Alan Haimes and Mario Mele, who eventually obtained controlling interest in the company. Joseph Alston was employed by DDS as a marketing representative. Alston was also involved with John and Joseph Martorano in Med-Bus, Inc. (See page 25.)*

**In 1974, Garner, then president of Garner Laboratories, a King of Prussia Cosmetics firm, was barred by the Pennsylvania Securities Commission from being associated with any security broker, dealer or investment officer, or offering the sale of securities in Pennsylvania for four years. This probation resulted from an investigation alleging fraud that had been perpetrated upon public investors regarding Garner Laboratories.*

**An employee of DDS informed the Crime Commission that, while Schiller and Sheller were listed as marketing agents, they were never actual employees of DDS. They were listed as marketing agents reportedly so they could receive a finder's fee if DDS secured a contract.*

Marketing Techniques

The Crime Commission's investigation showed that, during negotiations with unions for four separate contracts, AHP used questionable marketing techniques. This was found in regard to Teamsters Local 169 in Cornwells Heights, the Pennsylvania Social Services Union, AFSCME District Council 33 and the Philadelphia Fraternal Order of Police.

The cornerstone of AHP's marketing techniques appeared to be the awarding of so-called 'finders fees' to persons who were affiliated with the unions or had some influence in union leader's decisions. These 'finders fees' ranged from an alleged $600 payment to a Local 169 shop steward to a 14 percent commission on the AFSCME contract which went to a company owned by Peter J. Serubo.

Dr. Charles Kravitz also entered into business associations with several individuals who were closely associated with the contract award or who apparently had a connection to the people who controlled the contract award.

Following are the details.

Local 169

One of the first contracts AHP received was for the employees of Commonwealth International Incorporated, which later became Leaseway Warehouses Incorporated. Leaseway is located in Cornwells Heights and employs about 70 members of the International Brotherhood of Teamsters Local 169.

The Commission has uncovered evidence that the shop steward for the local union received a "finders fee" for his role in ensuring the award of the contract to American Health Programs, Inc.

The principal negotiators on behalf of AHP for the Leaseway contract were Dr. Kravitz, Robert Fluehr, and William J. Graf, Jr. (See Cast of Characters)

Graf testified that the chief negotiator for Leaseway was James Wise, a Local 169 shop steward. He further said that the approval of the health plan contract by the company was considered only a formality.

Graf was questioned further by the Commission and made the following statements:

Q: Was any offer of money or anything of value ever offered to anyone in the awarding of this contract?

A: Yes . . . at the suggestion of Dr. Kravitz, six hundred dollars was offered to Jimmy Wise as a compensation for the additional time put into the contract on behalf of his people. At that time we were informed by Dr. Kravitz that that would probably assure us the contract on any other basis, and he asked me to give Jimmy Wise a check for six hundred dollars, which would be reimbursed from American Health Programs, which never was . . . Actually, initially we were talking to him about more than that. In fact, Dr. Kravitz suggested a thousand dollars, and I refused vehemently about that and said, "No way." And he suggested six hundred, and that was what was given to Jimmy Wise . . .

Q: . . . who authorized the offer to be made?

A: Well, Dr. Kravitz talked with myself, Mr. Fluehr, and the three of us talked about it. We, Mr. Fluehr and myself, had objected to it. Dr. Kravitz reinforced the importance of a contract. We agreed to it . . .

Q: How much was paid to him?

A: Six hundred dollars.

Q: Who paid Mr. Wise the money?

A: I wrote him a check from my account.

Special agents of the Pennsylvania Crime Commission confronted James Wise with the allegations presented and Wise vehemently denied that he had received any fee for his role in the award of the contract. During a second interview with Crime Commission representatives, Wise was shown a copy of the cancelled check and at that time admitted that he had received the fee. Wise further acknowledged that pursuant to the agreement, he was to have received an additional four hundred dollars.

Although Wise stated that the offer of this money was never made to him personally by Dr. Kravitz, it is clear that Graf had paid this money in an effort to secure the dental benefit contract for AHP.

PSSU

AHP's first major contract for services was with the Pennsylvania Social Services Union, Pennsylvania Employment Securities Employees Association (PSSU/PESEA), which represents about 12,000 Commonwealth employees.

In October of 1975 PSSU's health and welfare fund trustees considered contracting for health care services with one of four providers. Among the health plan proposals was one from AHP.

The trustees' counsel, Steven Sheller, suggested in January of 1976 that expert advice be sought in evaluating the varied proposals.

The following month, Peat, Marwick, Mitchell and Company, an accounting firm, presented an evaluation of the four plans presented, plus two others. That report made some negative comments about AHP's plan, including the following:

"The apparent higher costs for participating dentists, the lack of consistancy between the Group Prepaid allowances and coverages and the insured Plan, would tend to make this proposal unattractive. This does not appear to be a vehicle which can offer maximum control of costs to either the Fund or the individual employee."

As a result of this report the board of trustees authorized legal counsel for the joint Commonwealth trustees, to enter into negotiations with Blue Shield.

Shortly after AHP was notified that it had not received the contract award, Eileen Kerlin, a union trustee, began to speak out on behalf of AHP.

On March 2, 1976, Kerlin advised the board of trustees that she had been contacted by representatives of AHP, who stated that they had been misrepresented by Peat, Marwick, Mitchell and Company. As a result AHP was allowed to submit a second bid for the contract. On April 2, 1976, the trustees approved the content of the new AHP bid, but decided to withhold actual approval of the contract until the Martin E. Segal Company could review the program.

In an eight page letter to the board of trustees, the Segal company stated:

"If we were the consultants to the board, we would recommend that this agreement not be executed in its present form."

The analysis went on to note:

"We add only one more point . . . We believe that the nature of this program as set out in the contract participating and non-participating, different benefits provided in each, unclear and unmeaningful prevailing fees, etc.— will make it difficult if not impossible for such a clear and concise statement of benefits to be made."

AHP, however, had retained Berle Schiller, Esq. in its attempt to secure the contract. Schiller, who had also been involved in DDS, had practiced law with Steven Sheller, PSSU's counsel. AHP's Director of Professional Relations, Dr. Sanford Roth, summarized Schiller's role in his immunized testimony:

Q: Now, you mentioned Berle Schiller. What was his role in this contract, attempting to secure this contract?
A: Okay. He knew a Steve Sheller who was an attorney . . . I think he was at one time in Berle Schiller's law firm—that was involved with the unions in terms of benefits or negotiating for benefits, and that's how we got the appointment to go speak as one of the possibilities for a dental contract.
Q: What was Mr. Sheller's position or function?
A: From what I remember, he was an attorney. I don't remember whether he was a union or Commonwealth attorney. If I remember, there were Commonwealth trustees, and there were union trustees there, which I don't remember.
Q: Was he present when you made your presentation?
A: Yes, he was.

On April 19, 1976, the contract between AHP and PSSU/PESEA was signed. Roth further testified that Sheller received a "finder's fee" regarding the award of the contract.

Q: . . . Was there what we have called a finder's fee in this particular contract?
A: Yes.
A: Are you aware of who received it and what the amounts were?
A: From what I remember, Berle Schiller got three percent, I got three percent, and Steve Sheller got three percent.
Q: It was a total of ten split three ways between Steve Sheller, Berle Schiller and yourself?
A: And myself.
Q: Why did Steve Sheller get a third?
A: I don't know that. I had nothing to do with it.
Q: Were those payments made directly by American Health Programs . . .
A: Yes.
Q: . . .to Steve Sheller?
A: To Berle Schiller.
Q: To Berle Schiller?
A: Yes.
Q: How did Steve Sheller receive his one-third?
A: That Berle Schiller was involved with . . .
Q: . . .How do you know that Sheller got a part of it?
A: After the contract was awarded, I was told that was the finder's fee.
Q: Who told you that?
A: Dr. Kravitz.

Roth was later asked how the fee was paid out. He replied,

". . .Berle Schiller got the total sum. He then obviously deposited that total sum in PNB, . . . and he would write Steve Sheller a check."

In addition to the testimony of Roth, the Crime Commission received similar information from a confidential source. According to that source, a 10 percent finder's fee was paid for the PSSU contract and that this fee was split between Roth, Schiller and Sheller. Schiller received approximately $22,700 as his part of the fee.

Berle Schiller denied transmitting any of the 10 percent finder's fee to Sheller. Sheller was subpoenaed to testify before the Pennsylvania Crime Commission but refused to answer any questions posed. In response to the question of whether he received any type of fee or payment in relation to the award of the contract, Sheller asserted the attorney-client privilege.

Regarding the commissions paid for the award of the PSSU contract, William Graf testified that AMARC was to have received a 15 percent commission for the award of this contract. Graf was informed, however, by Kravitz, Collier and Schiller that additional expenses had to be paid regarding this contract and AMARC would have to relinquish 10 percent of the commission to Schiller.

Graf testified regarding a meeting between Schiller, Collier, Fleuhr and himself, in which Schiller told the men why he would receive the bulk of the commission on the PSSU contract:

". . . He alluded to the fact that if the agreement (to give him 10 percent) were not executed, that in no way would we get that contract, that he was in—he was in a position at that point . . . to either make sure that the contract was awarded or not . . ."

Graf was asked if Schiller had told him how Schiller would prevent or allow the contract to be awarded and Graf replied:

". . . It seems that an attorney for the Board of Trustees named Steve Sheller . . . was to work out the details of the contract between himself and AHP, who was represented by Berle Schiller at that time. So the conversation alluded to the fact that he was working very closely with Mr. Sheller and, depending upon his attitude and how he handled it, would determine whether or not Steve Sheller would continue recommending the award to AHP or relating it to the Board that maybe it wasn't the greatest contract and they should look elsewhere."

Approximately one year after the contract award to AHP, the contract was terminated. Sources indicate that AHP lost the contract because the insurance agent who signed on behalf of Beneficial National Life Insurance Company (the co-insurer) did not have the authority to sign the contract.

From Trustee to Counselor

After the PSSU contract was over, Dr. Kravitz was involved in some personal dealings with Norman Hahn, who had been the chairman of the board of trustees of the PSSU during contract negotiations with AHP.

This serves as another example of an interested party benefiting from his relationship with AHP and must be considered a substantial conflict of interest.

After AHP was awarded the PSSU contract, Hahn was hired as administrator of the health and welfare fund at $32,000. He replaced Nathan Kolbes. The administrator is responsible for the daily operations of the fund.

In order to act as administrator, Hahn formed a company known as Fund Administrators, Inc., 13 North Progress Avenue, Harrisburg.

Between April and June of 1977, AHP disbursed four checks totaling $6,256.62 to Fund Administrators. One of these checks had the notation "prepaid consulting fee." The first of these checks was disbursed during the last month of the PSSU contract with AHP.

Hahn said that the money from AHP was for services rendered by him as an investment advisor. He stated he had purchased securities for Dr. Kravitz with money from a money market fund in Harrisburg. In return for his services, Hahn was to be given $3,000 each month.

Some securities were purchased in the name of the Philhar Company, located at the office address of Dr. Kavitz. Over $84,000 was involved in the Philhar Company account.

The Commission also learned that, during the fall of 1976, Hahn traveled to Tampa, Florida, at the expense of AHP, purportedly to discuss with Kravitz problems in the dental service contract.

AFSCME

Dr. Charles Kravitz met Peter J. Serubo in 1975, when Kravitz was President of Dental Delivery Services. He was introduced to him by Berle Schiller.

Serubo, who was at the time the owner of the Serubo Cadillac Agency, was purportedly assisting Earl Stout, American Federation of State County and Municipal Employees Union (AFSCME) President, in reviewing various prepaid dental care programs. Kravitz presented the DDS plan to Serubo but no positive action was taken by the union.

Two years later, after the formation of AHP, Kravitz outlined the program being offered by his new firm to Serubo and Stout.

One week later, Serubo informed Kravitz that he wanted a commission if AHP received the contract. According to testimony by Kravitz at a federal trial, Serubo requested 25 percent of the gross receipts that AHP received from the union. Eventually it was agreed that Serubo would receive a 14 percent commission.

An agreement was drawn up between AHP and Serubo's firm, Thomas Peters Management Company. This company, located in Jenkintown, had been formed by Serubo and his Cadillac agency partner, W. Thomas Plachter.

During the course of the District Council 33/AHP contract, Kravitz paid in excess of $600,000 in commissions to Serubo. Initially, the funds were disbursed to Thomas Peters Management Company, but later the commission payments were made to Dental Care Programs, Inc., another Serubo company.

In return for this commission, the Thomas Peters Management Company was to act as a liaison between AHP and AFSCME and organize, update, and verify lists of eligible union members under the plan.

While the agreement between AHP and Thomas Peters outlined the various functions to be performed by Serubo, the Commission has received information that his company did minimal work. Thomas Peters initially assisted AHP in obtaining the union member eligibility information but this function was eventually assumed by AHP.

The brochures that were provided to the union's eligible workers were paid for by AHP and District Council 33. It should also be noted that the Management Company was also to act as a liaison between AHP and members of District Council 33, regarding any problems that the members encountered with the dental program. The phone numbers to call, however, when a problem was encountered, were AHP's.

As a result, the $30,000 a month in commissions to Serubo appear to have been paid only for his role in helping AHP obtain the contract.

In addition to the monthly commission payment that AHP made to Thomas Peters Management Company, AHP paid an additional $15,000 to Peter Serubo. This money was paid in March of 1977.

After the signing of the contract, Kravitz paid for a trip to Bermuda for himself and his wife and for Peter Serubo and his wife. Kravitz testified that he did this because he was fearful that Serubo would have the contract taken away from AHP, and Kravitz wanted to create "good will".

In total, the Crime Commission found that approximately $600,000 of taxpayer's money was disbursed to Peter Serubo merely for his role of bringing Earl Stout and Charles Kravitz together. The work that was supposedly to be completed by Serubo's company, Thomas Peters Management, was minimal and for the most part never done.

FOP

In 1978, the City of Philadelphia agreed to a union contract which expanded its previous employee benefits plan available to members of the Fraternal Order of Police (FOP) and the Philadelphia Firefighters Association (PFA).

A committee was formed to review proposals submitted by health plan providers. This committee included representatives from the FOP and a representative from the PFA. The PFA subsequently decided to independently seek a health care provider.

According to a confidential informant, the committee decided that it did not want to deal with Kravitz after the second proposal, mainly due to the adverse publicity on him.

At that point in time, Kravitz utilized another contact to insure AHP's securing the contract. This contact was former State Senator Robert Rovner.*

**Dr. Kravitz was introduced to Rovner by Chester Weisinger. For more on Weisinger, see page 37.*
Rovner refused to testify before the Crime Commission when he was subpoenaed.

On behalf of AHP, Rovner made frequent calls to the members of the FOP and was successful in persuading the committee to give Kravitz another opportunity to obtain the contract. In fact, Kravitz appeared before the committee at least four more times. The other companies were only permitted two presentations.

For his services, Rovner was to receive seven percent of the contract or approximately $294,000. Originally, Kravitz had informed Rovner that the usual fee for such services was 15 percent; however, due to the fact that Kravitz purportedly had to pay other individuals, he could only pay Rovner half of the customary fee.

Some time around August 17, 1978, the committee decided to make the award to AHP. When the contract was awarded, no formal vote was taken, nor were any minutes kept of the meetings at which the proposals were discussed.

Interestingly, AHP was chosen to be the provider of dental, vision and prescription services even though the company had never been involved in the vision or prescription field prior to this time.

"Keep Him Happy"

Thomas Garvey, former head of the statewide Fraternal Order of Police (FOP), was a friend of Dr. Charles Kravitz, the owner of AHP. He was also, according to Steven Passin, former AHP President, ". . . one of the people that had to be kept happy . . ."

When Garvey heard, in 1978, that the Pennsylvania Crime Commission was investigating AHP, he voiced a continuing concern about that investigation.

Twice in 1978 and again in 1979, Garvey or his intermediaries contacted the Commission in an effort to find out what, if any, wrongdoing on the part of AHP had been uncovered.

He said he was concerned, on behalf of the FOP, about the proposed AHP/FOP contract and wanted to do what was best for the FOP.

Garvey may, however, have also had an interest in the welfare of AHP. On January 4, 1979, he incorporated Public Employees Consultants, Inc. (PEC) as its sole stock holder. PEC was located in Suite 1300 of the Payne-Shoemaker Building, 246 North Third Street, Harrisburg, PA. This location was the office of Attorney Gary Lightman, the individual who had been involved in the arbitration decision whereby the FOP was awarded a benefits package which included $4.2 million for dental and vision care contracts. Lightman was the attorney for this corporation.*

The Commission found that Garvey, for PEC, signed a marketing agreement with AHP on April 12, 1979. Under this agreement, PEC was to procure dental contract application for AHP. AHP advanced a total of $90,000 to PEC between April 1979 and February 1980.

In October of 1979, Garvey was interviewed by two Commission agents. Garvey stated that he had done a complete background on AHP prior to its selection as a health plan provider to the FOP and that he was completely satisfied with AHP. He further claimed that, apart from one unsuccessful transaction in Atlanta, he had not been involved in any business ventures with Kravitz.**

It was determined that, at the time of the Garvey interview, PEC had already received $70,000 from AHP, pursuant to the agreement.

In accord with the agreement, the money was "advance commissions" against money PEC would earn if and when it sold an AHP contract. In the event that PEC sold no contracts, the money was to have been repaid.

During the 18-month agreement between PEC and AHP, no contracts were sold. But, the money has still not been repaid.**

As a result of his PEC operation, Garvey received a salary of $15,090.95. He also received $3,000 for expenses, although this money was reimbursed. Information received also indicates that Garvey used PEC as a political base. Garvey was able to purchase sporting event tickets and entertain various political dignitaries. As an example, when a large number of Philadelphia Police officers were laid off, Garvey concentrated a lobbyist effort via PEC to enact a bill that would prevent this.

In addition to Garvey, PEC allocated $2,085.50 to the law firm of Davidson, Aaron and Tumini for legal fees. As the name indicates, this is the firm of Alfonso Tumini, the FOP attorney. PEC also paid a total of $4,400 to the Pinto Security and Investigative Systems, Inc. These payments were for background investigations on arbitrators. Joseph Pinto was a FOP member. The last corporate address of Pinto's operation was the law firm of Davidson, Aaron and Tumini.

In any event, AHP was responsible for setting Garvey up in business. Garvey resigned as president of PEC and transferred his interest to Paul Lightman, Gary's father, on April 11, 1980, 11 days after he was elected FOP President. There is no indication that Garvey was paid for his interest.

During the time period of mid-1979 to March of 1980, AHP employed Garvey's wife, Catherine, and Michael Pinto, the son of Joseph Pinto. Mrs. Garvey was paid $3,026.19 and Pinto received $8,121.33 for the three fiscal quarters.

*PEC also represented the Immediate Relief Association of the Pennsylvania State Police. This association was involved in supplying life insurance for the state police.
PEC also had an agreement to do labor work and consulting work for the 36,000 members of the statewide FOP. This could seemingly be a conflict of interest due to the fact that PEC could first get the municipality to pay for benefits, getting paid by the police for their efforts, and then try to sell the police the benefits getting paid a commission by the provider.
PEC also was attempting to organize casino guards in Atlantic City.*

*** Thomas Garvey was subpoenaed to appear before the Crime Commission but declined to testify on the basis of his Constitutional privileges.*

***It is interesting to note that PEC claimed it had performed services totalling $118,500. PEC then forwarded a bill to AHP showing the $90,000 received and showing a balance due of $28,500. Gary Lightman informed the Crime Commission that his bill was a ploy and it was merely forwarded to place AHP on the defensive.*

Utilization Reports

The Crime Commission's investigation showed that AHP significantly increased the figures in the utilization reports it provided to the Retail Clerks and AFSCME District 33. In both cases, the unions received reports indicating that they were saving substantial amounts of money.

AHP works on a capitation or fixed-fee basis with its dentists. That is, the dentists receive a fixed amount of money per family per month, regardless of the amount of services that family receives. However, the utilization reports show the value of services received on the basis of prevailing fees times actual services rendered, even though the prevailing fees did not represent actual payments to the dentists in this case.

These utilization reports, which AHP agreed to provide to its clients, were prepared by its staff. They also detailed the percentage of union members utilizing the service, the value of the services compared to the cost to the union, and the savings to the union and its members as a result of the contract.

Portions of AHP's utilization reports to AFSCME District 33 and the Retail Clerks Union can be seen in Appendix B. In summary, the AFSCME report, covering April 1 to September 31, 1977, showed 35,508 basic and complex services rendered with a value of $1,161,012. The Retail Clerks report, which covered August 15, 1976 to December 31, 1977, showed 31,809 basic and complex services delivered at a value of $1,622,800.

The Commission became aware that these figures were falsified when it obtained worksheets which were made up by Carol P. Lozanoff, an AHP employee. Portions of these worksheets can be found in Appendix A.

On these sheets, the discrepancy between actual services rendered and the number of services reported becomes obvious. In several instances in the AFSCME report, the reported figures were obtained by adding a round number, such as 1,000 or 2,000 to the actual figure. In the Retail Clerks report there did not seem to be any common percentage or pattern to the increases.

The discrepancy between actual and reported figures in these two cases is graphically portrayed in the bar chart on page 00. It shows that the usage and value of dental services received by members of both unions was largely overstated.

In terms of percentages, the AFSCME reported figures were up to 20 times higher than actual. The reported figures in the Retail Clerks utilization report were up to 392 times higher than actual.

In total, the actual number of basic and complex services rendered to AFSCME was 23,373, a third less than were reported. The actual value of those services, $568,407, was almost one half of the reported $1,161,012. The actual number of basic and complex services rendered to the Retail Clerks was 7,366, less than a quarter of the reported 31,809. The actual value of those services, $247,071, was less than one sixth of the reported $1,622,800.

Of further interest in these utilization reports is that they do not reflect the cost to AHP of these services, since AHP paid the dentists a fixed fee per family per month rather than prevailing rates.

The Commission could not, therefore, determine what AHP's actual costs for dental services were, what the administration of the plan cost, or what profits AHP made. As will be seen later in this chapter, however, it is interesting to note that Dr. Kravitz and Ms. Lozanoff received a total of $379,300 in loans and bonuses from the company in 1977 and 1978, on top of their $70,000 salaries.

The Crime Commission learned of AHP's inflated reporting from a former employee, Dr. Merwyn Landay, who testified that Carol Lozanoff had told him the figures were altered. He testified that:

"The actual services rendered were far below what the benefits were, and the premiums were coming in and were very low, and of course American Health Programs didn't want that reported. In a series of discussions with Carol, she began to show me these documents, the documents she was keeping showing the actual services rendered, what they were reporting, and she showed me this, and it became clear to me that she was reporting inaccurate utilization figures it seemed to me.

When I asked her why she was doing it she said that she carried the actual figures in, to the best of my recollection, and I think she was told they were too low to report, and as I remember it, she was being directed to, by Charles Kravitz, to change the figures. What the exact conversation was, I wasn't privy to that."

According to the Landay, Lozanoff had been "greatly troubled" by this practice and approached him:

Q: What was her specific problem when she came to you? You mentioned that she was having problems with these figures; what was her problem?

A: I think she wanted to know how to do this without doing it, how to do this without using two sets of figures which she couldn't do. Here her problem was, that she had given, as best as I can remember, she had given Kravitz a very accurate utilization report to be submitted to his accountant for cost and fees and she was being told that they were too low.

Q: How do you know that?

A: I think she told me that. I think the way it was, the words were, we can't send them in like this, something like that. She said that to me.

Q: What was her response to you?

A: "She showed me what the real problem was she was dealing with, and that was a real problem; how can she construct a utilization report that was closer to what Kravitz wanted to see. I guess that was a falsification of data and that was what she was struggling with."

Landay also gave some insight into how the figures were derived:

Q: Was she working backwards from the dollar figure to arrive at the number of services?

A: Yes, that was my understanding.

Q: By dividing the total dollar figure by customer, by the prevailing fee?

A: Yes, that's my impression, yes. At least coming close to the figure that was in somebody's mind that was the perfect figure to put in there.

Q: You said that it was your impression. Did she explain this to you personally?

A: Yes. In so many words, yes.

Q: She told you that's what she was doing?

A: Yes.

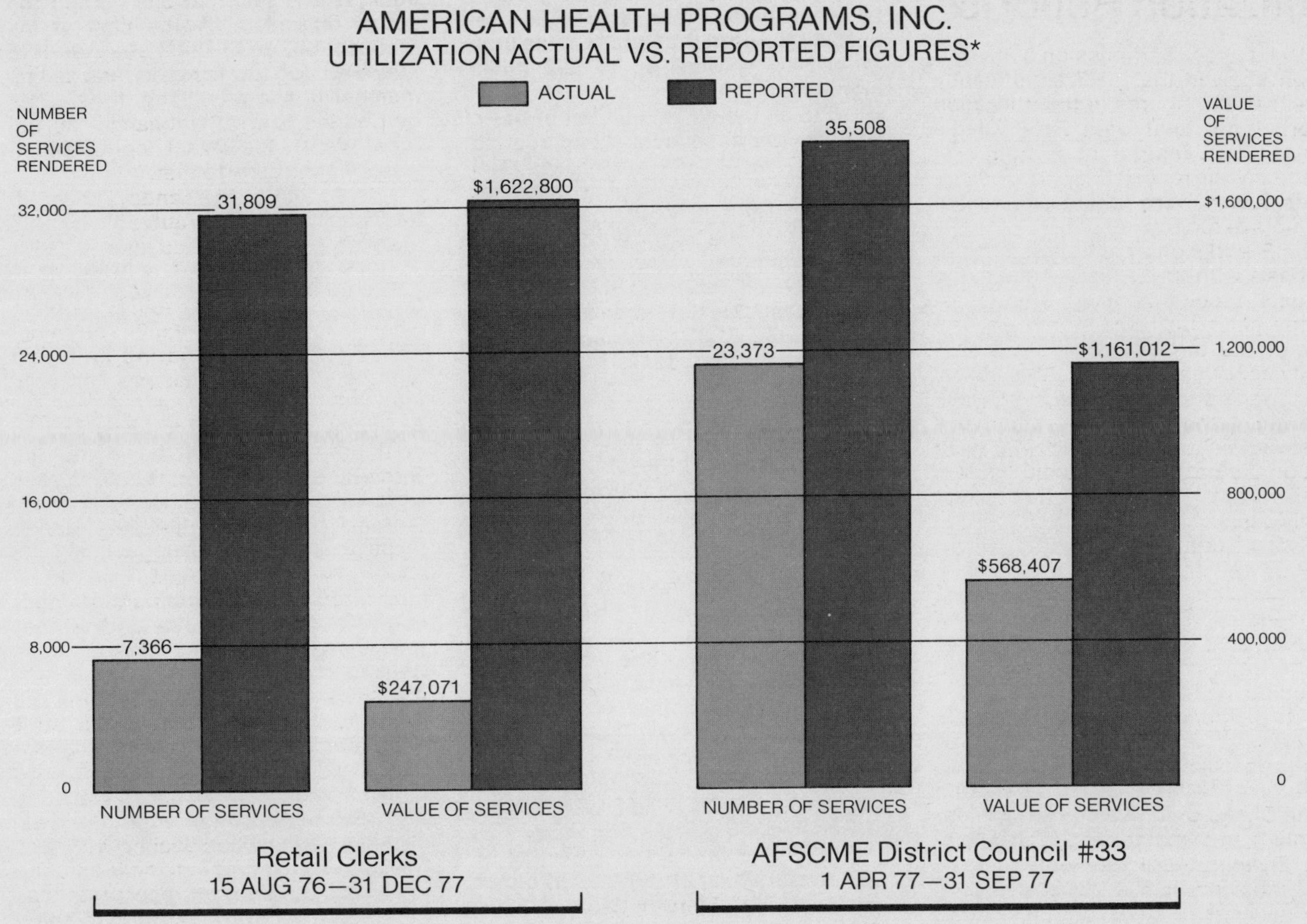

*Figures pertain only to basic and complex services; specialty services are not included.

The Crime Commission also subpoenaed the former president of American Health Programs, Inc., Steven Passin. While employed by AHP, Passin also learned of the inflated utilization reports. He commented that:

"The most irregular, and I don't know about illegal, but certainly the most irregular operation going on there was the falsifying utilization reports records so that they were—so that they represented what the client wanted to hear."

Passin also told the Commission who had been aware of the increased utilization figures:

"Carol Lozanoff, Len Alessi, Len Ostroff knew about it. But Carol Lozanoff was the person who Dr. Kravitz directly instructed to have that prepared in that way. She brought me a report she wanted me to approve. When I asked her how the numbers were constructed, she just laughed. She said, 'Don't you know? We don't construct them. We back into them. We get the numbers from Dr. Kravitz, what he wants to say, and create the data and we back up.' As far as Dr. Kravitz was concerned, that was the report that would cover everything. They could never go back and check."

Passin was asked if Carol Lozanoff told him directly that she falsely fabricated the reports under the direction of Dr. Kravitz. He replied, "That's right."

** Dr. Charles Kravitz invoked his Constitutional privileges in refusing to testify before the Crime Commission when subpoenaed.*

Lozanoff's Role

The Crime Commission subpoenaed Carol Lozanoff to testify. Lozanoff appeared, testified and answered various questions but refused to answer many of the questions asked based upon her Fifth Amendment privilege. As a result, the Crime Commission obtained a grant of immunity for Lozanoff.

Even under this grant of immunity, Ms. Lozanoff was hesitant to answer questions and detail the method by which she prepared the utilization reports.

Although she acknowledged the fact that the figures had been increased from the totals that had been reported by the dentists to AHP, she testified that the increased figures were reached through an extrapolation process.

At first, Lozanoff explained that she used a 15 percent error margin formula when compiling the utilization figures. She could not, however explain how, when, or where this error margin was used. Lozanoff further explained that the figures had been increased through the use of ratios. However, once again she was unable to give specific examples of how and when such ratios would be employed. She did testify that the increases of the utilization figures never exceeded 15 percent.*

When she was asked if she had "backed into" the figures, she hesitated and did not answer directly. When the question was restated, however, she admitted that she had.

Q: Is it not true that you backed into some of these figures by dividing a total dollar amount given to you by the prevailing fee to arrive at the total number of services? I think you understand what the procedure is.
A: Yes, I do.

After a consultation with her attorney, Lozanoff testified:

THE WITNESS: The answer to your question is yes.

Q: All right. Who gave you the dollar figures?
A: Dr. Kravitz.
Q: Who told you to arrive at the figures in this manner?
A: Dr. Kravitz.
Q: And what did he tell you when he gave you the dollar figures and gave you the instructions?
A: I don't know. Just . . .
Q: Well, why did he tell you . . .
A: . . . just the total should be X.
Q: Why did he tell you to do this? Why were you doing it in this manner?
A: So that the value of services would be more than the prepayment that the fund had paid us.
Q: And why would you do that? Why would you want to do that, and why was it done?
A: So that our reports would look acceptable to the people we were presenting it to.

A: And, yes, there were numbers changed as directed by Dr. Kravitz.
Q: He told you that it did not look good enough . . .
A: That's right.
Q: . . . and that it had to look better for the unions . . .
A: That's right.

**In reality, some figures were increased as much as 600 percent.*

Q: And it was done for both contracts, the AFSCME District Council Thirty-three and the Delaware Valley Fund, the two reports that we have shown you?
A: Yes.

Barland's Role

The Commission also subpoenaed Libby Barland, another former employee of American Health Programs, Inc., who was aware of the inflation of utilization statistics. Testifying under a grant of immunity Barland affirmed that the utilization figures had been increased from the figures that had been reported to AHP by the participating dentists.

Q: How did you cope with the problem of what you considered to be under-reporting by the dentist?
A: How did I cope with the problem of under-reporting?

Q: What remedy was proposed in order to correct the problem?
A: The remedy was to bring the figures up to a realistic rendition of what the figures should accuratey reflect.

Q: When you were coming up with accurate . . .
A: Accurate projections.
Q: Accurate projections, how did you do it? You are not a dentist; right?
A: That's correct. Very unhappily is how I did it.
Q: Would you explain that comment.
A: When I handed in figures, I always handed in actual figures for whatever services were performed. It was not a really pleasant experience to have them turned back and said this is too low to turn it into the union for the number of people involved and the number of services that should be reported.

Q: I think one question we really haven't answered before was the basis or the foundation that you used, or the knowledge of whatever you used to come up with the realistic figures when you were changing figures.
A: That was guesstimated projections as to what they should be.

Q: How would you guesstimate?
A: We sat down and tried to make determinations as to how many people actually went to the dentist, and how many had services rendered, and what the services should reflect.
Q: You are telling us what you did, but you are not telling us how you did it.
A: By pulling numbers out of the air.
Q: You pulled the numbers out of the air?
A: Based on standards, based on experiences, based on ADA books. But that is basically what we did.

Q: In other words, you fabricated the figures?
A: Embellished, if you will.

Barland was asked specifically how various figures for both the District Council 33 and the Retail Clerks contract were "embellished."

A: Depending upon what the actual figure was that was reported, and depending upon how many people actually went to the dentist. And then we guessed how many people should have gone to the dentist in the period of time and were not reported. And then we came up with a figure.

Q: Would you just add two thousand to it, or would you try to come up with some formula so it would come out to you saying, well, we are going to add five hundred and seventy-eight?

A: I don't remember ever using a formula. It was strictly looking at the figures, looking at the number of patients and the numbers, and guessing what really should have been reported.
Q: So, basically, it was a guess?
A: Yes.
Q: Did you ever increase the figures to the extent they were two or three times what was reported?
A: I would have to say yes to that. I don't actually have figures in front of me, but I would have to say yes, maybe on one or two services.

The Commission attempted to determine from Barland why the figures were increased:

Q: Would it be a matter of concern if the total value of services rendered was less than the premiums received from the union?
A: I'm sure that would have been a concern. I'm sure that's why the total number of services were increased.
Q: Was that specifically told to you? Was that the major consideration, or was that part of why the figures had to be projected?
A: I don't remember. I don't remember because it was basically because the utilization was too low, or because the services rendered were not high enough to justify the existence.
Q: Justify the existence of what?
A: Of the contract.

Conflicts

Both Carol Lozanoff and Libby Barland were subpoenaed to appear before the Pennsylvania Crime Commission during the public hearings that were conducted by the Commission.

During her public testimony, Lozanoff became evasive, contradictory and attempted to retract her prior statements. She once again explained that she arrived at the reported figures using an extrapolation process. She, however, could not recall what that process was. She could only say that it was based upon her experience and the data that had been received from the dentists by AHP. When asked what experience allowed her to make such extrapolations, she testified:

> "I have worked in a dental office from 1972. I had experience filling out insurance claim forms, reviewing patient records. I had done a lot of reading, research, consultation with doctors and patients."

But during the same public testimony when asked why she had previously testified that she felt increasing the figures was wrong, Lozanoff testified:

> "At the time that I felt it was wrong, I was upset. I had very little knowledge and didn't understand the logic. I didn't have a great deal of experience, and I gathered that experience."

Regarding her prior testimony before the Commission, Lozanoff testified at Pennsylvania Crime Commission public hearings that she did not understand the questions asked of her at that time. She indicated during the public hearing testimony that she did not understand during her prior testimony what the term 'backing into figures' meant, even though the question had been asked five times and explained in a way that was understood by her and so acknowledged.* Lozanoff, as noted earlier in this section did, in fact, acknowledge that she backed into the figures, yet in her public testimony she indicated that she did not and gave her reason as a lack of understanding of the question.

During her private testimony, Lozanoff also testified that Dr. Kravitz had given her the dollar figures that were to be reached and she testified that Kravitz had instructed her to use this procedure. During her public testimony, she denied that Kravitz had given her figures.

She did, however, reaffirm that the reason the figures were increased was so that the value of services rendered under the AHP program would be more than the prepayment which the health and welfare fund paid to AHP.

Dr. Charles Kravitz refused to testify, in private or public hearings, before the Pennsylvania Crime Commission.

During the Commission's public hearings, other representatives of American Health Programs asserted that the utilization reports were compiled in accordance with the standards of the dental industry and in any event such reports were not a material factor with regard to the dental program that was in effect for the two unions.

The Union representatives and trustees, however, were never informed of the changes that had been made in the utilization statistics. In addition, representatives of the Retail Clerks Union informed the Commission that these reports were one of the elements that the union would need and want in determining the benefits that are supplied under the program and the terms for the continuance of such a program.

During her private testimony, Lozanoff was asked five times if she backed into the figures and the term was specifically defined as obtaining the figures by "dividing a total dollar amount given to you, by the prevailing fee to arrive at the total number of services." Lozanoff was asked if she understood what was being asked and she responded, "yes". In addition, Lozanoff apparently wrote the question down and then consulted with her attorney regarding this question.

It is interesting to note that, in 1978 when the Tri-State Health and Welfare Fund was reviewing the performance of the North American Dental Plan program (See Chapter 1), they retained a consultant who, in part, was to review the utilization of dental services including a comparison of the cost of services against the capitation rate paid to the provider and to further determine the retention of premium which is not actually spent on dental services.

Weisinger's Deals

Chester Weisinger was involved in a number of investment transactions with Charles Kravitz and Carol Lozanoff which never appeared to bear a good return.

On December 7, 1977, Kravitz and Lozanoff transmitted a total of $70,000 to Atlantic Financial Services, Inc., at 1950 Street Road, Cornwells Heights. This financial consulting and brokerage firm was operated by Chester Weisinger.

Weisinger testified before the Crime Commission that the $70,000 was a loan to be used for real estate developments in Harrisburg, Lancaster and York. In return for the loan, Kravitz and Lozanoff were to receive interest and three percent of all profits derived from the sale of the developments. He further testified that the loan was not invested but was used for the day-to-day expenses of his business. The loan was never repaid.

Kravitz and Lozanoff also entered into a deal with Weisinger for $75,000 each whereby they would obtain ownership of 2.5 percent of the producer's share in "Terminus", a major motion picture. This proposed movie was to be produced by Premru Productions, Inc.

Weisinger claimed to have owned 30 percent of the producer's shares through his company, Atlantic Financial Services. Premu Productions had asked Weisinger to find financing of $2.4 million for the movie, but Weisinger was unable to do so. Weisinger was then asked to get $150,000 for 'pre-production' costs but told Premru he was unable to do so. Weisinger testified before the Crime Commission that he used the $150,000 invested by Kravitz and Lozanoff for his everyday business expenses.

Glen Premru, of Premru Productions stated that Weisinger would have received 30 percent ownership in the movie's production if he arranged for full financing, but the agreement was not finalized. He indicated that Weisinger did not have the shares, nor did he have the authority to sell the shares to anyone else.

Once again, neither Kravitz nor Lozanoff attempted to secure the return of the $150,000 they had "invested" with Weisinger.

It was reported by the Crime Commission in 1971 that Weisinger was intricately involved with Michael Grasso, Jr., a nephew and business associate of Philadelphia La Cosa Nostra leader Angelo Bruno.

Moreover, Weisinger was indicted by a federal grand jury in Chicago in February, 1972, in the Church of Christ Manors fraud, an advance free loan scheme which utilized phony loan commitments from Church of Christ Manors, Inc., a company purporting to represent Churches of Christ throughout the United States. Weisinger was acquitted of all charges.

Appendix A Evidence

The Pennsylvania Crime Commission's investigation showed that American Health Programs (AHP) Inc. substantially inflated the figures it provided to union groups in its utilization reports.

A portion of the AHP's report of Basic Services rendered to AFSCME District 33 members between April 1 and September 30, 1977 can be seen on page 39. Column 2, headed "Total # of Svcs. Rendered," is the key column in this report.

Also on page 39, there is an accurate reproduction of a worksheet prepared by Carol P. Lozanoff which the Commission obtained. This worksheet also pertains to AFSCME District 33 over the six months mentioned above.

The worksheet contains hand written numbers referring to actual and reported services rendered.

Under the column titled "Prevailing Fee," two sub-columns are marked "A" and "R". These stand for 'actual' and 'reported.' By comparing sub-column "R" in this report with column 2 in the utilization report, we see that the figures are identical.

A comparison between sub-columns "A" and "R" shows that the figures in "R" are inflated over those in column "A" in nine of 15 cases. On line two, for example, the number 944 becomes 2,994. On line seven, the number 156 under "A" becomes 1,156 under "R". The total amount of basic services under "A" was not added up on the original sheet, but comes to 20,208 services rendered. The reported number of basic services rendered was 29,589; almost a third more.

The utilization reports for the Retail Clerks Delaware Valley Health and Welfare Fund show similar disparities with their companion worksheets. A portion of AHP's utilization report to the Retail Clerks for the period of August 15, 1976 to December 31, 1977 can be seen on page 40. Once again, column two contains the reported number of services obtained by union members through the plan. Also on page 40 is an accurate reproduction of another Lazonoff worksheet which covers the 16-month period of the Retail Clerks contract.

In the column headed "Aggregate 16 mos." once again sub-columns of "A" and "R" are seen. The figures shown in column 2 of the utilization report are again identical to those in sub-column "R" of the worksheet.

A comparison between the figures in sub-columns "A" and "R" show that each of the 19 line items increase from "A" to "R". On line 11, a '1' in "A" becomes 392 in "R". On line 2, the number 271 in "A" becomes 1,370 in sub-column "R."

The totals at the bottom of the columns measure the great discrepancies between "A" figures and "R" figures. The "A" column adds up to 6,034 or less than one-quarter of the "R" sum of 24,646.

In all cases, these reports of services rendered were then multiplied by prevailing fees. The dollar amounts which resulted were then reported to the unions as the value of the services received by the unions. Because these usage figures were inflated and, consequently the value figures were inflated, the unions believed that they were receiving more services at a higher value than was actually the case.

The Commission determined that AHP reported approximately $1,968,332 in value of services that were never received by the members of three unions over a short period of time.

AFSCME District Council 33
Utilization Report Figures

ervice	Prevailing Fee	Total # of Svcs. Rendered	Worksheet Figures Prevailing Fee #1 6 MOS APR. - SEPT [illegible], '77 A	R
ASIC SERVICES				
Clinical Examination	10	4,350	4350	4350
Complete Intra-oral X-rays	28	2,994	994	2994
Individual Periapical X-rays	3	2,813	2813	2813
Bite Wing Series	11	1,897	1897	1897
Panorex	23	333	333	333
Study Models	13	1,606	60	1606
Treatment Planning	--	1,156	156	1156
ub- DIAGNOSTIC SERVICES otal		15,149	10603	15149
Prophylaxis	15	2,532	2532	2532
Fluoride Treatment	15	1,824	824	1824
Comprehensive Disease Control Prog.	30	1,127	127	1127
b- PREVENTIVE SERVICES tal		5,483		5483
Silver Filling - 1 Surface	12	3,087	2805	3087
Silver Filling - 2 Surfaces	20	2,430	2230	2430
Silver Filling - 3 or more Surfaces	27	1,778	570	1778
Plastic	35	145	NA	145
Composite Resins	24	1,517	517	1517
b- BASIC RESTORATIVE tal		8,267		8957
TAL BASIC SERVICES		28,899		29589

Retail Clerks Union
(8/15/76—12/31/77)
Utilization Report Figures

Service	Prevailing Fee	Total # of Services Performed	Worksheet Figures: AGGREGATE 16 MOS #4 A	R ✓
BASIC SERVICES				
Exam and Diagnosis	10	3,631	1073	3631
Complete Intra-oral X-ray	28	1,370	271	1370
Individual Periapical X-rays	3	1,902	615	1902
Bite Wing Series	11	2,190	590	2190
Panorex	23	311	100	311
Study Models	13	90	22	90
Treatment Planning	10	2,030	49	2030
Sub-Total DIAGNOSTIC SERVICES		11,524	2720	11524
Prophylaxis	15	2,629	770	2629
Fluoride Treatment	15	1,356	196	1356
Control Visits	30	850	61	850
Nuva-Seal (Sealant Treatment)	24	392	1	392
Sub-Total PREVENTIVE SERVICES		5,227	1028	5227
Silver Filling - 1 Surface	12	2,820	807	2820
Silver Filling - 2 Surface	20	2,747	752	2747
Silver Filling - 3 or more	27	1,156	360	1156
Composite	24	998	298	998
Pin Amalgam Restoration	8	28	12	28
Pin Composite	8	19	9	19
Nuva-Fil	35	117	45	117
Gold Inlay	150	10	3	10
Sub-Total BASIC RESTORATIVE		7,895	2286	7895
			6034	24646

Appendix B Fratianno Testimony Excerpts

The Pennsylvania Crime Commission held public hearings on July 28, 29 and 30 in relation to health care plan organizations. On July 28 at 1 p.m., Aladena "Jimmy the Weasel" Fratianno took the stand.

Fratianno came heavily guarded by U. S. Marshals. The self-admitted La Cosa Nostra member and hit-man has been in the Federal Witness Protection Program since December of 1977.

As was seen on earlier pages, Fratianno had personal knowledge of Labor Health Plans, Inc. operator Angelo Commito, and aided Commito in his attempts to secure health care plan contracts in Ohio (see page 18) and California (see page 18).

Following are some of the other statements made by Fratianno during his testimony.

La Cosa Nostra

Q: Have you ever been a formal member of an organized crime family or La Cosa Nostra?
A: Yes, sir.
Q: And what family was that, sir?
A: The Los Angeles Family I started with.
Q: And what was the title of that family at the time you started with them?
A: Well, Jack Dragna was the boss. They called it the Dragna Family, La Cosa Nostra.
Q: Now when did you become a member of the Dragna Family in Los Angeles?
A: It was either in late 1947 or early 1948.
Q: All right. Now how does one become a member of a recognized Cosa Nostra family?
A: Well, there's a lot of ways. You can be a son of a made member, which is easy to get in that way. You can be a relative. Or you have to be proposed. Somebody has to vouch for you.

And it might take a year, two years before you get in. As a rule, you've got to do something in order to become a member.
Q: Now when you became a member in 1947 of the Dragna Family, did you become a member after being proposed?
A: After I was proposed, yes. Maybe a few—four, five months after I was proposed I became a member, sir.
Q: Who proposed you into that family, sir?
A: Johnny Roselli.
Q: Did you have to do anything special to become proposed?
A: No. Just to have their trust. And they would check your background and inquire about you, from where you're from.
Q: When you become a made member, I assume that is a term that means that it separates the members from someone else, when you use the term "made"; is that correct?
A: Yes. When you're made, you're generally in the family.
Q: Now when you became made, sir, did you have to go through a traditional ritual?
A: Yes, sir.
Q: And could you describe what that ritual was?
A: Well, at the time I got made there was five of us got made at the same time. They take you in one at a time. You hold hands. They stand up. They lock hands. They have a long table, such as this; real long. They have a sword and a gun crossing one another.

You hold hands. Then the boss says something in Italian. It lasts maybe two, three minutes. And after that they prick your hand with the sword or with a pin and draw blood. Then you kiss each member on the cheek and they introduce you to each member.

Then they give you rules later. They tell you what the rules are.
Q: Now who is present during the proceedings of this ritual?
A: Well, practically the whole family. Whoever could attend, you know.
Q: Is it ceremonial within the family, the process of being made?
A: Yes. It's like a ceremony. In some states they have—cities, they have big dinners, after the people are made. Some don't.

You know, they have like a little party.
Q: Now is there also a code of silence?
A: Yes sir. Omerta.
Q: What is that?
A: Well, they call it omerta; silence. The code of silence.
Q: Is the 'omerta' described at that ceremony at the ritual?
A: Well, they explain all the rules to you. I mean I'll more or less tell you a few of them.

You are not allowed to speak to any agencies of any kind; FBI, any law enforcement. You can't answer no questions in no grand juries.

You can't fool with anybody's family, their wives or anything like that.

You cannot indulge in narcotics. They're very, very against that.

Q: Is that the use of narcotics or the sale of narcotics?

A: The sale, selling, dealing in narcotics or using narcotics. Them are some of the rules, the main rules that they tell you.

Q: Those are the rules that were told to you in 1947?

A: That's correct, sir.

His Role In La Cosa Nostra

Q: Did you ever move up in the ranks from within the Dragna Family?

A: Yes. In 1952 I became a capo.

Q: And had you done anything special between '47 and '52 to elevate you to that status?

A: I did quite a bit of work, sir. Yes, sir.

Q: What kind of work?

A: Well, up to that time I personally participated I think in four killings, another one in '53.

But that—I participated actually in five. And I did other work, you know, like putting a bomb under somebody's house.

Q: Okay. In 1954 you were sent to prison; is that correct?

A: That's correct, sir.

Q: For what offense?

A: Conspiracy to extort.

Q: Where did you serve?

A: I served approximately six and a half years in California.

Q: When you came out of prison did you still have the title of capo within the Dragna Family?

A: Well, as far as I knew, yes.

Fratianno further stated that he had asked to be transferred to the Chicago Cosa Nostra family in 1960 or 1961. In order to get permission, both family heads had to agree. Fratianno named Sam Giancana as the head of the Chicago organized crime family and Frank DeSimone, whom he said was an attorney, as the leader of the Los Angeles family.

In 1975, he asked permission to be transferred back to Los Angeles. The Cosa Nostra bosses involved in that decision, according to Fratianno, were Louis Dragna in Los Angeles and Joey Aiuppa in Chicago.

Murder Etiquette

Q: You testified that you participated in a number of killings or hits while you were a member of the Dragna Family. Could you please describe to us the procedure for authorizing a hit? Who if anyone must authorize that hit?

A: Well, the boss has to authorize any hit.

Q: When, from your experience, sir, when someone from within a family is hit, do you have any experience as to the probabilities of where that hit could come from?

For example, could a member of one family hit a member of another family?

A: No, sir.

Q: Why not?

A: It's just against the rules.

Q: In Philadelphia in the last year allegedly there have been—there have been several murders of alleged organized crime figures from within what has been known as the Philadelphia Family.

Would you have an opinion as to where those hits would have had to come from?

A: Right in the family, sir.

Q: Why is that?

A: Well, because that's the way it works. I go back thirty-two years. And I ain't never heard of a man from another family kill somebody in another family, unless they would ask for help.

Q: Okay. Now elaborating on the point that you made, that in almost all situations a, when a family member is murdered, that it is from within that family, is it also your experience that it is not uncommon that after a family member is hit there is some retaliation from within that family also?

A: Absolutely.

Q: So that there may be a series of murders from within one family. So that it's all intrafamily related?

A: It's happened many a time, sir.

Q: In the book, "The Last Mafioso", written about you, it indicates that you personally directly were involved in eleven murders and indirectly in twenty-five. Many of those murders were members of your own family. Is that not correct?

A: (No response)

Q: Some?

A: Some.

Q: In fact, the Bompensiero murder was a member of your own family, was he not?

A: That's correct, sir.

Q: And Bompensiero himself was a very close friend of yours, was he not?

A: That's correct, sir.

Q: In fact, when you and he were in prison together in California, you worked together inside the prison walls. Is that not correct?

A: Well, we were together. But we didn't work together. We was in the same prison.

Q: He helped you when he was a clerk, when you came to that prison?

A: Yes. That's right. Yes.

Q: And notwithstanding that relationship, you would have been compelled to carry out the execution of Bompensiero if you were so requested by the boss. Is that correct, sir?

A: Yes. That's correct, sir.

Q: Now relating that to the Philadelphia situation, and I think you've said you felt that the Philadelphia problem was one from within, an internal problem, it would therefore not surprise you that members of the former Bruno Family were executing each other, and that is the reason for this series of killings; is that correct?

A: That's my opinion. That's correct, sir.

Q: But if another family who were close to, for example, the Philadelphia Family, were asked by the boss or underboss, or whoever was in charge at the time, to assist in a contract killing, they would do that?

A: I don't get what you mean, sir. You mean if—let's, let's . . .

Q: Say a New York Family was asked to assist in a contract killing of a Philadelphia member by the boss of the Philadelphia Family.

A: Oh, yes.

Q: They would do that?

A: It's happened many times. Yes.

Q: Many times. And Los Angeles and Cleveland cooperated, just as Philadelphia or New York might have?

A: Exactly. Exactly.

Presser's Connections

Q: Yes. You indicated that Mr. Presser was owned by organized crime, and that the way that that occurred was that organized crime helped to pave the way to him ultimately becoming the Vice-President of the International Teamsters.

Could you detail for us, as much as you can, the ways in which organized crime was helpful in terms of assisting Mr. Presser in his career?

A: I—well, this goes way back, you know. See, Bill Presser, I knew Bill Presser when he was working with jukeboxes.

They eventually stepped him in a position where they could make money with him.

Q: Bill Presser was Jack Presser's father?

A: Jackie's father. That's correct. And then when his father retired, they put Jackie Presser in there. Well, his father told him what he's got to do.

See, there's a man in Cleveland that handles Jackie Presser, without the family knowing anything about it.

Whenever they wanted to see Jackie Presser, whenever I wanted to see him, we'd go through this, this fellow in Cleveland, a guy by the name of Rockland. Machie is his name. Machie. I forget his last name. Rockland or—but—now you asked how they get involved with the Teamsters.

Well, I was one of the founders of the Teamsters in 1929. There was twenty-five hundred members, Italian people who actually formed the Teamsters, if you go way back in the twenties.

And they've had it ever since. How do you think Hoffa got in there? Do you think he got in because his name was Hoffa? I introduced Hoffa to Joe Blimpobo, one of the heads of La Cosa Nostra in Chicago.

And they were against Hoffa. And this was in 1952, during the convention at the Statler Hotel in Los Angeles. I introduced him to the guy in La Cosa Nostra. The following five years, after bringing him in, Hoffa got in to be president. Hoffa did. How did you think he got in?

So it's the same way with these international vice-presidents.

Look at Roy Williams. Do you think he's there because his name is Roy Williams? So I'm just trying to tell you how it works.

Q: In your judgment does organized crime continue to have the same influence today in International Teamsters?

A: Absolutely. More.

Q: Why do you say "more"?

A: Because I know. You say how do I say it. I know who runs Roy Williams. They all have a man. They all have somebody that looks after them. And in return they got to give some favors.

Q: Who does run Roy Williams?

A: Nick Civella, Joey Aiuppa, Tony Giordano out of St. Louis. They're all bosses. They started Roy Williams, going way back. In fact, Bill Presser is the one that nominated him for international vice-president back in 1961 or '62.

Who do you think Bill Presser is? He was told to do that. How do you think Tony Pro (Provenzano) got in there? Because his name is Tony Pro?

You know, I'm just trying to explain to you how these things work. And you asked me how do I know. I've been a member for thirty-four years. I'm one of the originators of the Teamsters Union, going back to 1929.

The Casinos

Q: . . . do you have any opinion as to what if any influence organized crime has in the New Jersey casinos?

A: Well, I know they got some involvement. Because I heard talk when I was in New York.

There is involvement in New Jersey, although maybe it's hard to find. They use front men. How you going to find out?

Q: What do you believe is the nature and type of involvement that they have?

A: They got somebody there that's probably got a piece of it.

Q: Why do you think that?

A: Well, I don't say every casino now. Because that's the way it works. I know how it works in Las Vegas. Same thing. I know that there's other, other ways of making money; garbage.

There's a lot of ways. Selling them slot machines. There's a lot of ways of making money.

Q: Could you describe for us some of the ways that organized crime has made money in Las Vegas that might be areas of interest likewise in New Jersey?

A: Skimming. Skimming money out of the casinos. There's so many ways. I mean it's pretty hard to, you know, tell you how. There's so many ways to take money out of a casino, it's just unbelieveable.

You could take it from the slot machines. You could take it from the office. They can throw money at you when you're playing. There's so many ways.

Somebody can come in and win eighty thousand. That ain't no money in these casinos. Nothing to win eighty, a hundred thousand.

Success and Violence

Q: I have just a couple questions. Mr. Fratianno first you mentioned that several of the older members of the families had millions, many millions of dollars, untold millions.

A: That's correct.

Q: What, in your opinion, are the two or three primary reasons why they have been so successful and why the organized crime activities, the traditional family activities, have been so successful in making money criminally, and how do you see it in relation to law enforcement efforts?

A: You mean how have the crime elements been so successful?

Q: Yes, sir.

A: Well, it dates back to years ago, when they founded it, when they started it. Politically they do—like in New York, they got everything going there. They got the garment industry, they got the skylock, they got the numbers, they got everything.

Q: They control everything, is what you're saying?

A: They control it. That's correct. One family controls the trucking industry, another family controls the garment industry. It's different things. So in a period of years you, you accumulate a lot of money.

Q: How do they maintain and protect that enterprise? How do they control that inflow of money?

A: What do you mean, how do they control it?

Q: How do they protect or continue it on constantly, generally speaking?

A: Well, who's going to bother them? If somebody bothers them, they'll find themselves in the lake, in the ocean, you know.

Q: So violence does become the ways and the means, is the bottom line, so to speak?

A: I say if they have to. But people know what they're doing. You know, they ain't going to buck anybody. They know what's going to happen to them.

The Bruno Family

Q: You personally sir, have you had any direct involvement with any of the Philadelphia members, the members of the Bruno Family?

A: Yes, I have, with one. But he, I think he's died in the past year.

Q: Who was that, sir?

A: "Freddie Red Shirt." His name is Freddie Felice. He's with the Bruno Family. He's been with the Bruno Family for years. And in 1976 and '77 he was selling artichokes to New York.

Q: And you worked with Mr. Felice, "Freddie Red Shirt" Felice?

A: Yes, sir. We were partners, sir, also with Terry Zappi.

Q: In the right-hand corner of this chart they have three names up there; Sonny Franzese, James Calandrillo and John Allu. Do you know of any of those individuals?

A: I know of Franzese, but I don't know him personally, sir.

Q: Other than Fred Felice, did you have any personal involvement with any other members of the Philadelphia Family?

A: Well, years ago. Yes.

Q: Who was that?

A: With Blinky Palermo. That's going back a lot of years.

Q: At that time was he a member of the Bruno Family?

A: Yes, sir.

Q: Anyone else?

A: That's about it. Anybody that I knew quite well. I met Frank Palumbo years ago.

Q: Through whom?

A: Through Blinky Palermo.

Q: Frank Palumbo, the restauranteur?

A: Yes, sir.

Q: Was Mr. Palumbo a member of any family, to your knowledge?

A: No, he wasn't a member, sir. Blinky was a member.

Appendix C
Remarks of Doctor Alan E. Berger, Vice President of Health Care Services for American Health Programs, Inc.

Mr. Charirman, members of the Commission, Commission Staff, ladies and gentlemen:

I thank the Pennsylvania Crime Commission for permitting me the opportunity to appear voluntarily and address certain matters that have been presented at the hearings today. The purpose of my presentation is to clarify a misunderstanding that I believe exists concerning the value of utilization reports in a capitation program.

Capitation Defined

Capitation programs are defined by the American Dental Association as an alternative approach to the fee for service method of rendering professional services and dispensing remuneration to the professional provider. Capitation programs cannot and should not be evaluated by guidelines of fee for service programs. It is a system by which the participating dentist is compensated at a fixed per capita rate, usually on a monthly basis, in return for agreeing to provide specific, predetermined dental services as appropriate and necessary to eligible subscribers. Payments made by the American Health Programs, Inc. ("AHP") to the dentists are based upon the number of persons assigned for dental treatment during the length of the contract whether or not the enrollees use the dental services during this period. There is no correlation between the dollar value of services rendered and the dollar amount the provider receives.

Data Gathering

Capitation benefit programs do not require the submission of pre-authorization forms, bills for services rendered, or other claim forms which are required for payment of services in an insured program. The professional provider or dentist is often remiss in providing details on services he has rendered as the information he is requested to furnish AHP (the administrator) has no bearing on the dollars he earns. The method of gathering data, the compilation and the interpretation of that data must by necessity be different.

Our own experience and frustration in trying to gather accurate data has been substantiated by Dr. Max Schoen, Chairman and Professor, Section of Public Health and Preventive Dentistry, U.C.L.A., the acknowledged expert on capitation programs. Dr. Schoen has stated,

> "Where no bills or claim forms are required for payment the dentist often is reluctant to tabulate details on services with any degree of accuracy. A developing network must use a combination of persuasion and withholding of payment (or a portion thereof) to bring participating offices into compliance. By the time a system has matured or stabilized, this problem should be overcome, but several years may be involved. In the interval, estimates must be used which are based on samples of offices which are known to be reporting accurately, and selected samples of other offices. Data are then extrapolated to approximate the level of operation of the system."

In the early years of operation, AHP as an emerging organization experimented with a number of reporting techniques which had been developed in order to properly obtain information concerning our program. Two problems immediately were apparent: many participating dentists did not provide reports of the services rendered and, of those who did, the reports were largely incomplete and contained obvious aberrations of data. With this in mind, a number of methods were developed to provide our Operations Department with sufficient information on which evaluations can be made, using the techniques recommended by Dr. Schoen such as withholding payment and not assigning new patients to a facility.

Utilization Reports

Utilization reports containing the compilation of specific services rendered and the dollar value of those services are relevant only in insured fee for service programs as administered by an insurance company. An insurance company must have this information to determine its premiums and its financial exposure or risk. If the risk is high, the premium goes up or the contract is cancelled.

An increase in demand for services such as crown and bridge, prosthetics, orthodontics, etc. means greater financial exposure that the insurance company must face when administering a fee for service reimbursement benefit plan. A determination must be made of the value of services rendered by the dentists versus the amount of premium paid. Based on these figures, deductibles are determined and premium rates rise or fall.

In a capitation program utilization reports are not relevant. AHP is marketing good oral health and is not interested in determining how much fee for service dental care can be provided. Utilization in a capitation plan means generalized use—how many members and their families are availing themselves of the benefits by requesting and accepting assignment to the dentists and thereafter following up this assignment with a visit as the beginning of their treatment which will insure good oral health.

The analysis of compiled data is also different in a successfully administered capitation program because the number and value of services performed should decrease as patients are treated into a state of good oral health. In essence the dollar premiums received in a capitation program should eventually exceed the dollar value of service rendered. This fact allows capitation plans to legitimately claim that they are cost effective. As Dr. Schoen has stated, the *value* of services rendered is immaterial in a capitation program since *"capitation rates are not based on the total of 'fees' produced."*

The important statistic then for the client in a utilization report is *useage.* We want useage to be high in the sense of the members availing themselves of the services provided, in order to initiate treatment and promote good oral health. Our goal is to arrive at a maintenance level as quickly as possible.

We have honored our pledge to our clients to take steps to promote useage. Our Operation Department continuously evaluates, along with the Marketing Department, ways in which to promote optimal use of services, and in this vein provides information for client publications, meetings with shop stewards, and seminars to acquaint members with the services which are available under their benefit program. Pamphlets and brochures are developed for members defining the specific areas of coverage and steps for using their benefits.

In summary, under our plan no utilization reports are necessary because it is a capitation, not a fee for service reimbursement system. We are providing prevention and good oral health. We are not marketing dental services. If one understands the value and concept of capitation, one then would see that to increase the value or number of services rendered in a utilization report would be self-defeating.

Internal Use of Utilization Reports

A capitation program should collect data on general utilization of the benefits, as well as on the quantity and distribution of services. This information is valuable to us as the administrators for internal use only. When properly compiled it allows the consultant staff of AHP to analyze, evaluate, and compare the performance of the different doctors within our participating network. What we look for is a ratio between different services performed. For example, how many extractions versus root canal procedures to determine the preventive orientation of an individual practitioner. As stated by Dr. Schoen,

> "over a period of time the incidence of extraction should decrease both in absolute numbers and as a percentage of restorative services. Diagnostic and preventative services should increase as a percent of total services."

Our internal use of utilization and procedural reports has enabled us to administer a viable Quality Assurance Program conducted by our consultant staff which includes:

a. Procedural audits
b. Analytical audits
c. Clinical audits
   1. selected offices and patients
   2. specialty pretreatment screenings in orthodontics and periodontics
d. Peer review when necessary

Conclusion

During the six years AHP has administered prepaid dental capitation programs, we have by necessity been innovative in our approach as there were no generally accepted precedents to follow. We have come to realize and accept the fact that the material we gather and compile under a general heading of utilization must be corrected and extrapolated to approximate the level of operation within our system. Our earlier reports to member groups included a conventional utilization report in addition to capitation utilization. This was done purely to share the information available without any intention to mislead. Indeed, artificially increasing the value or number of services rendered would be detrimental to the intended goals of the program.

We believe we have a system that is cost effective from the point of view of the client, be it a business, union, or governmental unit. The premium of our contract is fixed for the life of the contract (in some cases three years), and unlike insurance programs, which are experienced rated, as stated earlier, our program is one of the only where the premium is fixed.

Over the past years, AHP has offered assistance to Dental Societies and other agencies, including the Pennsylvania Crime Commission, in the creation and implementation of legislation surrounding dental plans in the Commonwealth of Pennsylvania. We welcome others in our emerging industry to assist AHP in establishing guidelines which will help standardize the health care benefit industry.

Index

The inclusion of a name in these indices does not connote criminal activity on the part of a business or individual.

Please check the page references listed to see the role of the business or individual in this investigation.

Government officials, commissions and authors are not indexed.

Businesses and Entities

Unions and Associations

Pennsylvania Crime Commission Published Reports 1969-1980

Task Force Report: Goals for Justice (1969)
Task Force Report: Assessment of Crime and Criminal Justice in Pennsylvania (1969)
Task Force Report Corrections in Pennsylvania (1969)
Task Force Report: Alcohol and the Criminal Justice System (1969)
A Report on the Inquiry into Gang Violence in Philadelphia (1969)
Criminal Justice Planning and Action in Pennsylvania (1969)
Comprehensive Plan for the Improvement of Criminal Justice in Pennsylvania (1969)
Report on Organized Crime (1970)
Report on the Conditions of Organized Gambling and the Administration of Criminal Justice in Johnstown, Pennsylvania: 1970-71 (1971)
Report on the Investigation in Delaware County, Pennsylvania, with Particular Reference to Abuses in Bail Bonding: 1970-71 (1971)
Criminal Infiltration of Legitimate Business in the Philadelphia Area (1971)
Report on Professional Crime in Pennsylvania (1972)
Report on an Investigation of Liquor and Penal Code Violations and Enforcement Policies in the Locust Street "Strip" Section of Philadelphia (1972)
Report on an Investigation into the Alleged Fixing of Certain Harness Races at Pocono Downs Track in 1971 (1972)
Gambling and Corruption in Phoenixville (1973)
Corruption in the Philadelphia Police Department (1973)
A Case Study of the Second Class Township Code—Chartiers Township (1973)
Investigations in Delaware County—Macing and Corruption (1973)
Corruption in the York Police Department (1974)
A Case Study of the Pennsylvania Election Code (1974)
Migration of Organized Crime Figures from New Jersey into Pennsylvania; A Case Study of Syndicated Gambling in Bucks County (1976)
Conflict of Interest and Self Dealing by Local Public Officials and Employees: Pocono Township, Monroe County and Marple Township, Delaware County (1977)
The Administration of the Criminal Justice System—Liberty Borough and West Mifflin Borough (1977)
Gambling and Its Effect Upon the Criminal Justice System—Patterns of Sentencing in Allegheny County Gambling Cases (1977)
Absentee Voting Irregularities in Delaware County (1977)
Fraudulent 'Cents-Off' Coupon Redemption Schemes (1977)
Abuses and Criminality in the Bail Bond Business in Pennsylvania (1977)
A Chester City Racketeer: Hidden Interests Revealed (1978)
Interstate Shipment of Gambling Paraphernalia and its Distribution and Sale Within the Commonwealth (1978)
Racketeering in the Casualty Insurance Industry (1978)
Macing and Extortion in the Pennsylvania Department of Transportation (1978)
Voting Irregularities in Philadelphia (1978)
The Penn State Group: A Study in White Collar Crime (1978)
Racketeering in the Commercial Loan Brokerage Industry (1980)
A Report of the Study of Organized Crime's Infiltration of the Pizza and Cheese Industry (1980)
A Decade of Organized Crime: 1980 Report (1980, second printing 1981)
Annual Report (1981)

All the publications prior to the *1980 Report* are no longer in print. Members of the public may obtain a copy of the *1980 Report*, at a nominal cost, through the State Bookstore, 10th and Market Streets, Harrisburg, PA 17125.